RESIN ART

A Step by Step Guide for Beginners

Tatiana Danilova

Artan Publishing

ARTAN
PUBLISHING

CONTENTS

1. ALL ABOUT RESIN

What is epoxy resin?

Epoxy resin is a synthetic oligomeric compound, a two-component polymer of a liquid consistency, consisting of a resin and a hardener. When both components are mixed, durable plastic-like material is formed.

The main characteristics of the resin:
- Strength.
- Heat resistance withstands up to 200C.
- High level of adhesion, the strength of joints to glue different surfaces.
- Waterproof does not absorb water when cured.
- Resistant to many chemicals.

Resin types

Resins come in different viscosities. This must be taken into account when choosing resins.
a) High viscosity resin.
This resin can be used for cuts of stones, since Geoda is ideal to come out, where clear lines are required.
b) Medium viscosity resin.
Designed for any type of artwork: abstract paintings, clocks, sea, bijouterie, Geoda stone cuts. It is convenient to make a finishing layer with such a resin. Its consumption is less. Suitable for beginners.
c) Liquid resin.
Designed for the finishing coat, for abstract paintings, for beginners who need a longer time to work with resin. There are liquid resins, the polymerization cycle of which is longer, up to several days. You need to ask manufacturers or read reviews.
d) Pouring resin for thick layers.
It is intended for filling transparent finishing layers, making jewelry. The difference between this resin and other resins is the ability to make castings from this resin up to 10 cm thick in one layer (check with the manufacturer).
e) Resin for jewelry.
It has a high degree of purity and is used for casting jewelry.
Thermal protective topcoat.
The resin for the protective layer is designed so that there are no scratches.
Ideal for cup holders, trays, tables. Such a coating has an elastic structure when the resin is applied to the product and smoothes very quickly. Heating can withstand up to 220g. And there is UV protection.

Stages of the resin-hardening process

• Liquid consistency. At this stage, you can fill in paintings, surface finishing layers, any shape.

• Resin is like liquid honey. At this stage, you can make a convex lens with a flat base.

• It looks like thick honey. At this stage of solidification, gluing objects is suitable.

• The epoxy resin cannot flow and the substance remains sticky.

• The "rubber" stage is when the resin does not stick to anything, but still bends like rubber. At such a moment, vases or any deformations can be made, fixing the resin in such a position that it does not straighten again.

• Fully cured resin. After drying, the resin becomes very strong.

The standard resin proportion is 1:10. There are proportions 2:1; 1: 40; 1:46; 1:85, etc. More often you can meet proportions of resin and hardener 2: 1. This means that you are measuring out two proportions of resin (component A) and one proportion of hardener (component B).

Each resin manufacturer has its proportions, do not forget to clarify if it is not written anywhere on the container.

2. SAFETY IN WORKING WITH RESIN

The harmfulness of epoxy is associated only with its liquid state. After hardening, the resin is non-toxic and harmless!

Inhalation of vapors in a liquid state may cause poisoning symptoms such as headache, cough, stomach discomfort, and allergic skin reactions. Volatile compounds produce toxic effects on the nervous system and liver. To avoid all this, you need to follow

Simple safety rules

While working with resin you will need:

• Respirator - mask or half mask.

Designed to protect the respiratory system from organic gases, vapors, aerosols, and dust when working with epoxy resins.

When working with small products and not often working with epoxy, you can use aerosol and anti-dust respirators with an exhalation valve, class a P3, which retain at least 94 -99% of harmful aerosols and dust. The same respirator is used when sanding the back surfaces of the resin.

For frequent work with epoxy, I recommend a respirator or half mask with replaceable filters to protect against harmful gases and vapors. Filters (cartridges,) must be of the A1, A2, and A3 brands. The letter A means that the filter is designed to protect against organic gases and vapors and the number indicates the protection class: 1 - low, 2 - medium, and 3 - high efficiency.

For example, I use a 3M 6000 mask + there are filters for a 3M 6000 or 3M 6200 half mask.

Change filters as you use the respirator. This mask can be purchased either in hardware stores or on the Internet. Disposable respirators cannot be reused.

 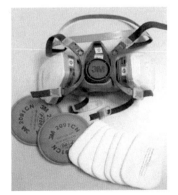 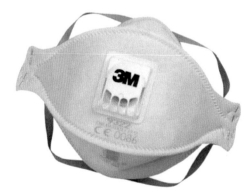

• Nitrile gloves
Hand protection from chemicals is MANDATORY when working with resin! Nitrile gloves are

completely hypoallergenic and more resistant to cuts. Vinyl gloves are the thinnest and most likely to break.

• Ventilated room!
It is not advisable to work in the kitchen! Remember that inhaling resin vapors in a liquid state is not recommended.

• Resin-proof apron.
Perhaps someone also needs armbands, but I work without them. You can simply choose regular clothing that is specifically designed to work with resin.

• Protective glasses.
They are necessary when processing a poured surface, for example, when sanding a painting. Resin dust during grinding can also get into your lungs, and on the mucous membrane of the eye, glasses will save you.

• Scrunchy. Our hair is attracted to the resin, so both the hair and the painting must be protected.

• You can drink an antihistamine if you know you have an allergic reaction to the resin.

Pregnant women and children under 15 years of age are not recommended to work with resin!

Create beauty safely!

A double pair of gloves is needed so that you can carefully remove the first ones when they get dirty with resin and not be distracted to put on new ones. When working with epoxy, food containers and silicone molds for cakes cannot be used, even "once". Also, there should be no food in your resin workspace.

3. MATERIALS AND TOOLS FOR RESIN ART

Materials

• Covering tape.
It is necessary to save the workspace. Use dense polyethylene, it will not tear during work. Greenhouse wrap or 120-liter thick garbage bags are suitable.

• Plastic cups (small, medium, large).
The container is designed for mixing epoxy resin. The container can be of different types:
1. Disposable cups (small, medium, and large will be needed).
2. Silicone cups (you need small, medium, and large).
3. Plastic hard cups. They do not bend, ideal for putting a tablet on them.
4. Any plastic containers for food.

• Wet wipes.
Any wipes containing alcohol. There can be any, my favorite Johnson's, they clean the resin better than other wipes they contain more alcohol.

• Wooden spatulas (small, medium, large).
Spatulas are needed to knead resin in cups and stir dyes and glitter.
We use wide and medium spatulas with 200-500 ml cups.

In large buckets (from 500 ml and more) we knead with a large wide spatula. You can take any suitable piece of wood (such as wooden ruler). We need small sticks for mixing resin in small cups (for example, we mix resin with glitter, liquid gold, etc.).

Big spatula 150mm x 18mm

Medium spatula 114mm x 10mm

Small spatula 140mm x 6mm

Multifunctional spatula

• Durable masking tape! (wide and medium).

The tape allows you to cover the back of your work and also serves to create the borders of the picture. The durable tape prevents the resin from spreading and smudges your paintings, making them aesthetically pleasing and neat.

Through trial and error, I tried different scotch tapes, but for working with resin I prefer Tesa's painter tape. I recommend to take masking tape 50mm * 25mm and 25mm * 25mm blue, yellow, or green.

Adhesive tape can be glued in different ways:

1. Making skirting (to control resin and beautiful skirting). The tape should be higher than the sides of the tablet.

2. Without skirting (for pouring the finishing layer). The tape must be glued from the sides and lowered down! With this placement of the tape, the resin will flow down without touching the underside of the painting. After the resin hardens the next day, you can easily remove the tape.

• Roller (small, medium) and brush - sponge.

Foam rollers and brushes are intended for priming the tablet. Any soft foam rollers and sponge brushes are used so that no marks remain on the surface and the bristles do not fall out of the brush.

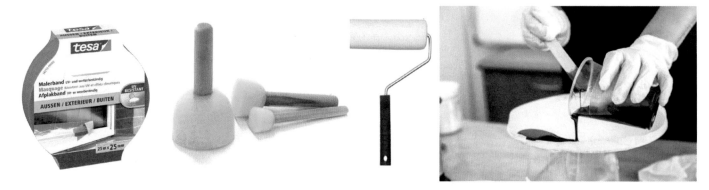

It is better to paint in the direction of the pile, holding the brush at a slight angle
- so there will be no brush marks. Do not forget to rinse your brushes out of acrylic paint immediately, otherwise, the brushes will be discarded.

Tools

• Hairdryer and burner.

The hairdryer is your brush for creating your design. You can move it, direct the resin in the direction you want. If you turn on the strong flow of the hairdryer, then you can mix your entire conceived drawing. Hot air dryers are good for creating waves in the sea.

The hairdryer is used with a construction (industrial) with attachments or an ordinary powerful hairdryer for drying hair with the hot air of various temperatures.

The burner quickly removes air bubbles that appear in the resin. When the two are mixed, bubbles form in your container. If your resin is a liquid or medium viscosity, the bubbles will go away on their own. If there are still a few bubbles left, then a burner can come to the rescue. You can purchase the Touch mini-burner.

Drive the burner quickly, without staying in one place and 5-7 cm above the surface, otherwise the resin may boil/turn yellow / form lumps and your product will be damaged!

• Scales.

Scales are necessary to strictly observe the proportions of the base composition and the hardener. The most common kitchen electronic scales will do. But electronic construction scales give a more accurate result.

• Waterpass.

A waterpass is needed to level our workspace so that the resin doesn't run down to one edge. By the way, if you don't have a level at home, you can always download the Waterpass application to your phone.

• Grinder (eccentric).

The machine (eccentric) is needed to sand the back surface of your products. Without it, no work looks so aesthetically pleasing.

When choosing a grinder (eccentric), pay attention to the possibility of collecting dust in a special container (dust collector). So that your dust does not scatter throughout the workshop (room).

the machine will need grinding wheels, grit 40 to 1800 + felt wheel for polishing.

• Dremel (multi drill) + accessories.

This machine is designed for polishing, milling, drilling products (for watches), and surface treatment in hard-to-reach places (Geode). It is advisable to take with speed control.

To drill holes, additional drills and collets are needed if there are none in the set. Choose drills with a cross-sectional diameter from 0.5 mm to 2.5 mm. An adjustable speed from 3000 will be sufficient for your products.

Dremel takes when you have been working for Resin Art for over a month.

• Painting brushes, artistic in various sizes.

They are also intended for priming the tablet and side ends. For painting the side parts of the product, for example, with liquid gold leaf.

Synthetic fiber brushes are better than natural brushes,

as their nylon marketing hairs tend to repel moisture. Take care of your brushes by rinsing with hot water and a little soap. This will help clear any broken fibers from the bristles. Then press and dry.

• Palette knives.

I use this tool to smudge resin onto my tablet to create beautiful textured effects. The palette knife for painting is more suitable for paintings using resin since the bending of the steel prevents the resin from accidentally touching your hand and spoiling the drawing.

A palette knife with stainless steel will last you longer than a plastic one.
It is better to wipe the resin off the palette knife immediately with alcohol wipes.

Construction goggles will serve to protect your eyes when sanding products. Small resin particles are harmful to the eyes.

Soak the brush to absorb moisture before priming your tablet. This way you will achieve a smoother and more even paint application.

Wrap the hairdryer, burner, and scales with cling film for a long look. Change the film as the resin dries the next day.

4. DYES AND ADDITIVES

Dyes

You will get more pleasure and opportunity by painting resin.

Dyes are needed to obtain a conceived drawing using the Resin Art technique.

using dyes, you can give the product the desired colors, create interesting transitions, and over-flows.

There are many different resin dyes on the art market.

• Liquid dyes.

There are dense and transparent dyes.

Transparent dyes are toners (tints), ideal for creating seas, jewelry, various inserts into a picture/product.

Dense dyes (non-transparent) are highly concentrated opaque dyes. They give a rich opaque color. About 30 ml of dye is enough for 4-5 liters of resin.

After mixing the resin with the hardener, add a couple of drops of dye immediately. Large amounts of colorant can cause the resin to not harden. The proportion of adding any colorants to the resin should not be > 7-8%.

• Pigments.

These are dry finely dispersed powders. They need a little more thoroughness and longer than dyes, mix well with the resin so that no lumps remain.

There pearlescent pigments that can be added to any shade and get interested in iridescent com-position. They look spectacular in the space theme and stone imitation.

There are pearl with blue, yellow, and white tints. Keep in mind, that this affects the color! Check with the manufacturer for the color of the pearl.

We do not put pigments into a glass over product . They are volatile and can crumble into your painting.

• Metals (pop-up powders).

They give a stunning effect of gold, bronze, silver on the surface of the work in the Resin Art technique.

Metallics are added to clear or colored resin. You can not stir the metallic in the resin, knock on the glass, tilting it to one side or the other. You will see a film of gold appear in the glass. If you don't want a film, you can mix it in resin, pour it onto the painting. The powder will float up faster if you go through the burner. But remember the distance, you can only walk with the flame not close to the surface.

You will see the gold pigment particles float up in thin threads.

• Acrylic paints.
Any thick acrylic paint will do. Add a little until the desired color is obtained. But it is better to use special resin pigments.

• Soap dye.
This dye makes the resin opaque if more is added than usual. Add a little, stirring, bring to the shade you need.

• Acrylic ink (Liquitex Acrylic Ink).
This ink has a beautiful palette. The resin color will be loose.

• Water-based building colors.
An economical option. You can buy it at any hardware store.
Add little by little, no more than 7-8% of the total.

• Alcohol ink.
If the ink is fully mixed with the resin, lumps may remain. Appear due to the uneven evaporation of alcohol. Applied in the Petri Art technique, which was invented by the artist Josie Lewis. Here it is important to catch the golden mean, to find the desired resin viscosity, since if the resin is liquid, the ink will immediately mix in it and you will not get beautiful stains. Resin has to be soft as honey. You will see the best results when using factory-made ink!

• Aerosol paint.
Metallic paints give very beautiful streaks. You can use graffiti spray both for creativity and ordinary ones that are sold in hardware stores. The palette of paints in spray cans is varied.
The seashore in the picture will perfectly come out using a spray can in gold color. We do the seashore with aerosol paint as follows: spray the paint at an angle onto the slightly hardened resin! From the edge of the picture to the shore, then a beautiful film is formed, in the form of golden sand.

• Glitters, sparkles.

Glitter can be added to both transparent and dyed resin. The effect of space is beautifully obtained by adding blue sparkles to dark shades.

• The ink from helium pens.

Very concentrated, very little resin staining required.

In general, any paint is suitable for epoxy resin.

• Pigment additives.

The main thing is that they are dry, or with a nitro solvent.

Do not rush to buy ALL resin colorants at once. It is enough to have the main primary colors: red, yellow, blue, and a lot of white. Colors should be free of impurities.

By mixing the primary colors, you can easily get a huge variety of colors: red + yellow = orange, etc.

When getting pastel shades, you need to add drop by drop the pigment to the white shade! and so on until you get the shade you need.

When mixing pigments, you can always look with a wooden spatula to see the natural color of the pigment that you will have on the tablet.

Additives

• Sea wave.

It is a white powder that is used with resin to create realistic sea waves.

It is necessary to mix thoroughly, otherwise small particles of white powder will remain in the picture when blowing with a hairdryer.

• Cell effect.

Serves to create cells and openwork film at work. Craters are created when the gel is created! Get ready for this. After drying, I cover it again with a transparent layer to get an even layer in the work.

• Natural stones, minerals, crystals, imitation resin stones.

Natural stones can be found on the Internet. Imitation of resin stones can be made using molds. With the help of them, you can create stones of the desired shade. To prevent the stones from drowning, it is better to sprinkle them when the resin has hardened.

• Glass crumb.

Glass can be of different fractions, consider when choosing from manufacturers on the website. Flower shops also have crumbs in different shades. In IKEA has beautiful white fine glass grit is universal for any paintings. White glass grit is versatile and can be colored.

• Fluorescent powder (with luminophore).

The powder can be added to the epoxy. Mix thoroughly. In the dark, your product will glow. Ideal to use for night lights, galaxy paintings.

• Potal.

Added and kneaded into the clear resin. The flaked leaf is suitable for cup holders and jewelry, for example. Ferrario liquid leaf is suitable for decorating epoxy resin works. Ideal for coloring the side of items (cup holders, trays, vases, etc.).

• Stabilized moss, shells.
It is used for marine-themed paintings.

• Sand.

Very fine sieved sand is added to the transparent resin. For example, for the coast with a marine theme.

• Dried flowers.

So that the dried flowers do not float, you need to pour the first layer, wait for a little, lay the flowers, and pour again gently on top.

The resin can not add fresh flowers, they fade right into the resin after a while.

Markers

With the help of markers, we can make outlines on our paintings/products, for example, Geode. Contours are made on a completely dry surface. Markers come in a variety of colors and thicknesses.

Markers with a medium tip - 0.7 mm, 0.8 mm, 1.0 mm, 2.0 mm are suitable for the Geode.

Adhesion to the surface is good; markers contain alcohol and water-based inks.

The palette of colors is large, but it would be nice to have basic colors in your work: gold, silver, bronze, white.

I recommend markers from the following manufacturers:
1. Pen-Touch, Edding,
2. Posca PC-1M,
3. Molotov Liquid Chrome (silver color, has a max mirror effect).

You can paint the mirror crumb with alcohol ink of any color!

Pour the required amount of crumbs into the glass, drip 3-4 drops of ink, cover the glass with a nitrile glove, and shake well.

5. SURFACES TO WORK

To work with resin, you can use surfaces such as:

- Small canvas
- Glass
- Mirror
- Organic glass
- Metal
- Clay
- Plywood
- MDF, laminated MDF
- Wooden surfaces
- Professional boards / tablets
- Surfaces painted with acrylic paints, oil, ink
- Photos
- Paper
- Plastic
- Plaster bas-relief
- Ceramics

Your bases can be of any shape (round, square, rectangular, hexagons, Geoda blanks), or they can be those that you can think of. Don't be afraid to experiment!

I like to use wood, namely birch. It has a high strength. The wood itself is light and pleasant to work with. It is easy to paint and resistant to cracking, which is important. Years later, you will be calm about your product.

The market also offers professional boards/tablet for drawing. For example, artboards.ru offers excellent drawing tablets, I use them in my work. These plates do not require priming and have beveled edges to help you achieve the perfect edges of our products.

If you use poplar, there will be a lot of bubbles in the work, even if it is primed. Very soft and porous wood.

6. PRIMER FOR BASES/TABLETS

A primer is needed to protect our surfaces and for better adhesion (cohesion).

For example, wood is absorbent and porous in structure. To prevent air bubbles from escaping, the villi of living wood must be "sealed" as it were. The epoxy is very liquid and will move at the slightest opportunity, and subsequently will bubble and be difficult to fix.

A good option if your substrate is white, opaque (so that the tree does not show through the resin). The white backing makes your paints look brighter and more expressive on the tablet. You can also prime the tablet with colored acrylic paints according to your drawing.

If you plan on painting with dark resin, it is recommended that you prime the tablet with dark acrylic to express the depth of your painting.

All wooden surfaces can be primed with any acrylic or building primer paint. An economical option is color paints in hardware stores.

The metal must be degreased with acetone, and then covered with an alkyd primer. Dries up to 24 hours.

Glass - the need to pass sandpaper for better adhesion/cohesion.

Professional tablets do not require a primer.

You can use any soft brushes, foam roller to prime the tablet so that no marks remain on the surface.

Resin does not like moisture! After priming your surface, wait until it is completely dry. Where the primer has not dried, and you have poured resin, the next day there may be a sticky layer or a matte area in that undried place.

Also, the primer can be dried with a hairdryer if needed quickly, but natural drying is encouraged.

When priming the tablet under the sea, I recommend doing stretching (gradient, smooth transitions) between colors. Then your sea will look real, without abrupt transitions.

7. RESIN CONSUMPTION

You must calculate the resin consumption before starting work. It should be enough to cover your work well, without stretching the last drop across the entire tablet, but with a small margin. A thin layer of resin will make your painting look too transparent.

Resin calculation is different for all manufacturers. Through trial and error, I found a middle ground using the formula:

The simplest formula for resin consumption:

$X * Y * 1.2 + 10\%$ = amount of resin, where

X = layer thickness in mm,

Y = area in m2

For thick resin, when the density is higher, it is better to use the coefficient 1.3:

$X * Y * 1.3 + 10\%$ = amount of resin,

where X = layer thickness in mm, Y = area in m2

Example:

Layer thickness X = 1mm

The area of our tablet is 50cm * 50cm = 0.25 sq. cm. Medium density resin (coefficient = 1.2) $X * Y * 1.2 + 10\% = 1 * 0.25 * 1.2 + 10\% = 0.33$ l. = 330ml

This means that 330 ml of epoxy will be required to work with a 50 * 50 cm square tablet.

The proportions of our resin and hardener are 2: 1 (each resin manufacturer has its proportions, please specify).

Divide the total amount of resin 330 ml by 3 and get:

component B (hardener) = 110 g,

component A (resin) = 220 gr.

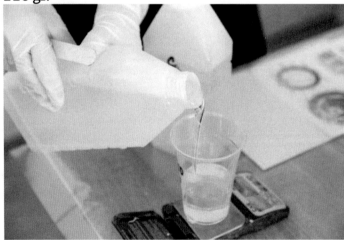

There are many electronic calculator sites on the Internet that you can also use.

Usually, every resin manufacturer has its online calculator for its resin.

8. APPLICATION OF EPOXY RESIN

Resin is used in various fields: in construction, industry, medicine, and other fields. Epoxy is considered a durable adhesive.

You can pour resin on almost any surface, for example, tables, cabinet doors, nightstands, beds, tiles, coffee tables, chairs, boards, large decorative panels.

You can also create works of art from resin:
- clock
- bijouterie (pendants, rings, earrings, etc.)
- decor elements and compositions
- decorative tiles
- photos, photo frames
- cup holders, candlesticks
- decorative items for weddings
- cabinet handles
- shelves
- decorative vases with a glowing ribbon
- bar counters
- tables, kitchen aprons
- dressers
- sculptures and many, many interesting things.

You can also fill the canvas with resin, but there are nuances.

The canvases are delicate, they can only be used in small sizes (up to 40 cm), since the resin, under its weight, will accumulate in the center of the canvas, exposing the stretcher and deforming your drawing.

Resin build-up can be avoided if:

1. Place the pressed foam on the inside of the canvas so that it fits snugly inside. Then you can cover the canvas on top with resin.

2. Pour resin over the entire inside of the canvas. After the resin is completely dry, pour as usual. In this case, however, a large consumption of resin is used.

Paintings can be filled with resin up to 5-8 layers. This will give the picture a special depth and originality.

The resin sticks to almost everything except galvanized steel, lead, nickel, rubber, silicone, and a variety of polyethylene (polycarbonate, plexiglass, etc.). Also does not adhere to greasy surfaces.

9. COMPOSITION IN DRAWINGS

For your painting to grab the viewer's attention, you need to understand the composition in the drawing.

The composition is the basis, the foundation of any piece. This is all that is around us, the arrangement of objects according to all the rules, which can help the viewer to correctly read what is conceived.

Resin paintings are mostly non-objective compositions. This format is very close to abstractionism.

The abstract (formal) composition is the absence of a theme, where we cannot see the clear meaning, but we can feel the author's mood by the colors, by the form, by the canvas on which the composition is based.

The abstract composition is based on juxtaposing straight, curved, or round lines, juxtaposing contrasts. Such paintings lose top and bottom, they can be viewed and turned from any side, they should not reflect reality.

Usually, a person tries to express the idea of a painting through objects. In our case, at the beginning of your creative path, a drawn diagram will help, in which you can use the most important composition rules.

Diagrams below we see the rhythm, that is, the alternation of any elements in a certain sequence, highlighting the key plot lines.

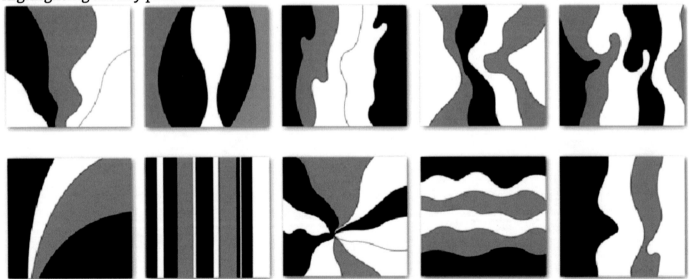

Our task is not just to pour resin onto our tablet (although this is also possible), but to observe some rules or principles of composition. Let's take a look at them.

One of the basic principles of composition - is a three-component, when you use three object quantities, three different directions, and three different colors, the picture is harmonious.

The compositional center is where the viewer's attention is drawn. This will usually be the most contrasting place in your painting.

The intersection point of the composition is called the geometric center of the composition. If you place an object in this center, it will look harmonious.

Using the Resin Art technique, the selection of the compositional center is associated with the help of color. Your subject will determine the light contrast solution of the visual center. In addition to the lines of the composition, it is important to consider the tone and color scheme that will convey your feelings and thoughts to the viewer.

On the diagram, you can see that in the compositional center there may be one main plot that attracts attention, or there may be several compositional centers at once. To give our paintings some dynamics, we can shift the composition center.

To create a feeling of lightness in the composition, it is better to make a contrasting spot just above the geometric center of the sheet.

It is better to use a vertical format.

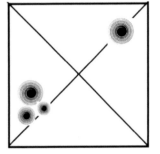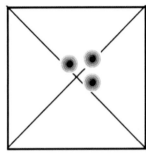

Composition rules

• The Rule of Third is the perfect tool for good composition. Divide the painting into 9 equal squares visually. To achieve a harmonious composition, place the composition center in the central rectangle.

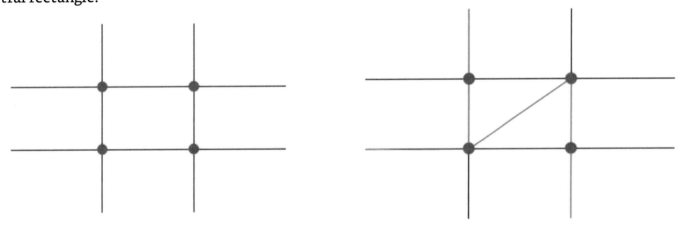

In the pictures above, we can see the sequence of reading points of attention by the human eye. Scanning the image starts from the top-left edge and continues along the red line. Our eyes perceive the image better by moving from left to right than from right to left.

To achieve balance in the composition, you need to shift the image to the right. You can use this knowledge to maximize user attention.

Specifically, I avoid symmetry in abstract paintings. I mentally make points of contact asymmetrically to make the work more dynamic and interesting. By making your resin lines well centered, you make the painting boring and uninteresting.

• The rule of the golden ratio is the ratio obtained by dividing the line into two parts, where the ratio of the greater part to the smaller part is equal to the ratio of the full line to the greater part.

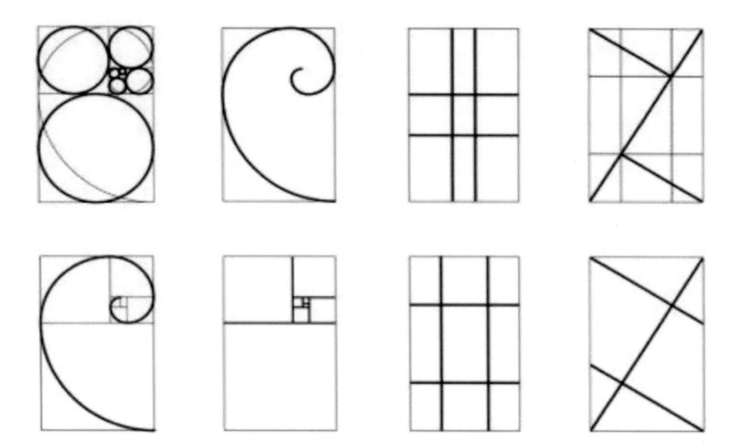

The diagram shows the types of the golden ratio: spiral and the diagonal golden ratio and the rule of thirds.

Clear your mind before using the resin. Try different application techniques and you will see which one you like best.

You can try not to think about the picture in advance, but just think about form or action before starting work. Mix paints and pour resin onto the tablet however you like. Get creative. Your emotions and imagination will be reflected in the picture.

For your resin paintings to look harmonious, not just one dirty spot, you need to learn the basics of color science. The color will be discussed in the next section.

Dark fills visually reduce the picture, light ones - on the contrary.
The round tablet format will give your painting a calm finish.
The rectangular format of the painting enhances the monumental impression of the image.
To prevent the picture from being oversaturated or too dark, you can leave more air, i.e. white.

10. PRINCIPLES OF COLOR

Color is important to the artist, as the correct application of colors is one of the conditions for a successful drawing. With the correct use of one color or another, you can convey a mood or evoke an emotional state of the viewer. A high degree of memorization is predetermined by the presence of stable associations associated with a particular color.

Basic color principles you need to know and understand.

Three properties of color:

• Hue - The name of the colors (for example, red, yellow, blue);
• Saturation is the pallor or darkness of a hue (color);
• Intensity - Determines the brightness and dimness of the hue (color).

The color wheel (Itten's circle)

It is a tool for combining colors. An excellent assistant in choosing colors for both designers, artists, and other creative people.
• Harmonious color combinations can be positioned against each other.
• Color combinations are evenly distributed, forming a triangle (Tetrad).
• The color combinations are evenly distributed to form a rectangle (Square).
Below is a color scheme for harmonious color combinations.

Basic color schemes

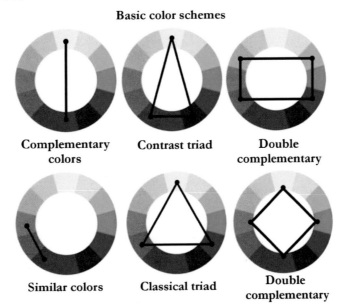

| Complementary colors | Contrast triad | Double complementary |

| Similar colors | Classical triad | Double complementary |

The traditional form of a color scheme is three primaries, base colors: red, yellow, and blue (also called primary colors).

When these three basic colors are mixed, secondary colors or colors of the second group are obtained. These include green, orange, and purple.

These colors are obtained by mixing the base primary colors. For example, red + yellow = orange, blue + red = purple (these are the secondary colors), etc.

By mixing each color with the adjacent one, we get six more colors of the third group color.

Color balance

If you only use one color or all the base colors in your work, then this work will look inharmonious and will not catch the viewer's eye.

Therefore, it is recommended to achieve a balance in your color composition, and namely: add a few colors of the third group or a little light shade of the same color.

Selection of colors, energy pictures

As Kandinsky said, human emotions can be conveyed only by color, without resorting to depicting real objects.

Before starting work, you need to think about the theme and color scheme. Imagine at once what result you want to achieve. The artist puts his emotions into his paintings, and the stronger the emotions, the more they are transmitted to others.

Color affects a person at a physiological level. Some colors can be soothing, others can energize us or make us feel comfortable, etc. Pale, desaturated shades, and the predominance of cold shades add thoughtfulness. Warm, rich tones create a more joyful, upbeat mood.

I will briefly describe the meaning and properties of each color, as a small tip.

• Red is the color of fire and passion. A bold, energetic, vibrant color that symbolizes confidence, strength, and power. Bright accents of red, for example, in the bedroom are recommended by sexologists, but it should not be intrusive, small blotches of red are ideal.

• Orange is the color of freshness, creativity, youth, and energy. This color is ideal for small spaces where there is little natural light. Since it is an appetite-stimulating color, it is suitable for dining rooms and kitchens.

• Yellow is the color of smile, positivity, joy, and light. Paintings with yellow color will visually add volume to small rooms. This color is also used for children's rooms.

• Blue - coolness, freshness, openness, freedom. They are used in classrooms and offices.

• Dark Blue - reliability, sociability, and openness. This color has a calming effect on a person. Helps to fall asleep quickly, but it suppresses passion. Dark Blue is preferable to use in restrooms, in meditation rooms. The deeper the blue color, the more the striving for the pure awakens in a person. For an English-speaking audience, blue may indicate depression, as in English, there is an expression " to be blue ", which means "to be upset, sad". Check before ordering.

• Green is a natural color, the color of life, environmental friendliness, wealth, and prestige.

It calms. Paintings in a dark green palette represent prestige, wealth, and abundance (malachite).

• Purple - spirituality, mystery, extravagance. This is the color of art, the color of women. Purple will look good in living rooms, but in bedrooms and dining rooms, it should be placed with extreme care, where there is a little purple, as it can restrain appetite and desire.

• Turquoise is an extravagant color, the color of life. However, this incredibly rich shade can be psychologically crushing if it is in excess, therefore it is recommended to dilute this color with another shade.

• Pink/purple - inner freedom, security, innocence, sentimentality, and romance. This color is a symbol of youth and creativity.

• Brown is the color of sanity, business relationships, and stability. Calm color, simple, evokes a sense of material security and self-confidence. Earthy shades can be used in any environment.

• Gray is a neutral color. It is believed that this color can help relieve stress while being practical and calm.

• Black is the color of luxury, sophistication, and sorrow. Black goes well with gold and white colors. Depending on the texture, your artistic message, idea can be changed. Perhaps the matte black elements in the paintings, together with the glossy surface, will look incredibly sophisticated.

• White - symbolizes purity, innocence, goodness, life, minimalism. Used with the visual expansion of the room, makes the room light. The transparency and perfection of this color always look winning. In a picture with more white, it will emphasize brevity, minimalism, simplicity, and luxury.

• Gold - symbolizes not the only luxury. It is considered the color of health, optimism, vitality.

• Silver - soothing, sensuality, and mystery. It is the embodiment of politeness, wealth, restraint.

• Bronze is a touch of luxury. Impeccable in ethnic style, ultramodern software, eclecticism, modernity, and minimalism.

Fashion trends in art and design can also be taken into account. *Pantone* color is determined every year. This can be a good hint for your future painting.

11. TEMPERATURE FOR WORK WITH RESIN

The recommended room temperature when working with resin should be slightly higher than room temperature, from 23 to 27C, but when working from 20 to 25C, the resin will also harden well.

In the winter months, I recommend pre-heating the room. Before starting work, also warm the resin in a water bath for 20-25 minutes if your resin is cold.

The first 24 hours of curing is critical, so the room must be kept warm and dry! (50% humidity), no temperature fluctuations.

You can display your work in the sun by the window. But at night I recommend removing from the window, as the temperature will drop sharply and the next day an "orange peel" may form in the picture.

The optimum storage temperature for epoxy resin should be at least 20C. The resin should be at room temperature. Containers with hardener and resin are stored in a dark place from direct sunlight. See resin label for resin shelf life. If stored in a dark place, the resin will last longer.

12. PROTECTING THE PAINTING FROM DUST

Your paintings and any resin products should be protected from dust as soon as they are finished. After work, the painting must be protected from dust particles. Vacuum and dust off before handling the resin in the area where you are working to reduce the risk of invisible dust particles.

There are various options for protecting paintings from dust:
• a dust shield in an art store,
• regular box by size,
• cardboard to the size of the picture,
• insect mesh screen cover,
• homemade box - protection made of wood/plexiglass and stretched film.

At high room humidity, dullness or matte spots may appear on the surface of the picture, mixed with gloss. It is possible to remove such stains after complete drying by sanding the surface and refilling with transparent resin.

13. ISSUES IN WORKING WITH RESIN

By weight or by volume?

We mix the epoxy resin with the hardener, according to the manufacturer's instructions (instructions are written on the resin packaging).

It was said above that there are proportions of resin and hardener 2: 1; 1: 1; 1:40; 1:46, etc. The instructions must be strictly followed!

Resin manufacturers usually indicate the proportion by weight, so you need to measure the components on a scale, and not measure by volume, this is important! If the proportions of resin and hardener are not properly proportioned, the resin will not cure, there will be a sticky film, etc.

The two liquids are thoroughly mixed until a homogeneous mixture is obtained. Stir by scraping off the sides of the container. Stir slowly to form fewer bubbles.

If the resin is a liquid or medium viscosity, then the bubbles that appear will come to the surface quickly and burst themselves, and with a thick resin, the bubbles remain where they were. We remove the bubbles with a burner.

Reasons why resin has become dim

The reasons for the turbidity of the resin:
• occurs due to moisture in the room.
• poorly mixed ingredients together. Stir longer until the resin clears.
• clouded when exposed to water. Resin is not friendly with water! Even a drop of water can have unpredictable effects.
• cloudiness or formation of a "crust" is possible even from accelerating the drying process using a hairdryer.
• do not mix different ingredients from different manufacturers. It can also lead to cloudiness and non-solidification of the resin.

Reasons why a product with time acquires effusion and flows

After a while, an influx of resin appeared in your painting. There may be several reasons:
• too thick applied to the product. Apply a thin layer of resin gradually. After curing, apply another coat if necessary.
• the room temperature is out of specification. Try to work at a higher temperature, above 23 degrees.
• the product was hung upright too early. Allow the last layer of resin to finally cure before hanging it on the wall. Usually 3-4 days.

Reasons why epoxy has boiled

Does the resin in the cup in your hand start to heat up quickly, or does the resin stick out? This is when two components are mixed, heat is released, a chain reaction occurs, and a fast polymerization process begins. Causes:
• large volume of resin has been mixed. Try to work with small volumes. Mix resin directly in a container with a large surface area.
• too thick resin applied. Apply a thin layer of resin gradually. After curing, apply another coat if necessary.
• added more hardener. Observe the rule of weight ratio.
• large amount of dye is mixed with resin (not more than 7% by volume). If the glass of resin becomes hot in your hands, place it in a container of cold water and stir immediately to dissipate the heat. If you missed such a moment, the resin begins to harden, then set the glass with resin away from you, as harmful toxic fumes begin to be released from it. It is no longer possible to work with such a resin.

Reasons why an amine film on epoxy resin

Sometimes spots appear on the surface that resembles a wax film. The reasons for its appearance are:
• work with a small batch of resin. With small volumes of resin, the required heating does not occur. Water ingress to the surface. Resin does not like water.
• the room temperature did not meet the standards. Leave the product to harden at a temperature above room temperature.
• use of pure butane when removing bubbles with a burner. It is necessary to fill the burner with a mixed type of gas - butane, and propane.

You can remove amine plaque by sanding the product and covering it with a new layer of resin after the resin has completely solidified.
If you do not sand the previous layer with the amine film, then there is a possibility of peeling and delamination of the second layer due to reduced adhesion.
I do not welcome the method of washing this film with water, since there is little effect from this, the resin loses its shine and you still have to cover it with a new layer of resin.

On the photo: Amine film on the product.

Reasons why epoxy resin does not harden

Typically epoxy harden after 24 hours, depending on the resin manufacturer.
The resin gains full strength after 72 hours.
If after 72 hours your product has not completely frozen, then the reason may be as follows:
• too much hardener. Observe the weight ratio.
• the resin with the hardener was poorly mixed. Stir for at least 4 minutes, scraping off the walls of the container in which you mix the resin.
• the room does not comply with the temperature regime, it is cold. The room temperature should be between 23 and 27 degrees.
• components expired. Pay attention to the expiration date of the resin.
• the resin is too thick. Choose the correct resin. If you need to pour a thick layer of resin, the art market may offer a special resin for pouring thick layers.

If you pour the resin in the hot months, I recommend that you put the container with the resin in cold water for 15-20 minutes before starting work so that the resin does not boil after mixing. The hardening time of the resin is reduced during hot months. Therefore, do not use quick resin during these months.

If you have large volumes, I also recommend placing the resin in a container with cold water. In this case, it is necessary to stir the resin intensively so that there is a heat sink. The chain reaction will not start (heating) if the components are colder than 25 degrees.

If you urgently need to run away for a while, and the resin is mixed, there is an option to pour it into smaller glasses and put it in the freezer. This will extend the life of the resin.

14. SILICONE MOLD FOR RESIN

There are a lot of molds on the market now, but not all molds can be bought, what to do?

Each silicone mold has its own expiration date. The better the silicone, the more fillings it can withstand. Therefore, after about 10-15 fills, your silicone mold loses its main initial qualities (scratches appeared on the product, the gloss was lost). If the silicone begins to stick to the resin, it has already worn out, you can part with it.

You can make Molds itself, use silicone rubber or silicone injection. The likelihood of bubbles will be less, the accuracy of the shape is higher, and it comes out cheaper with molded silicone.

Liquid silicone is a compound, a two-component composition that consists of a base substance and a hardener. The use of molding silicone is simple: you mix the silicone itself (A) and the hardener - catalyst (B) in certain proportions.

The proportions are different - 1: 1 (when two jars are the same in volume) or 100 grams of base and 2.5 grams of catalyst (2.5%) (when one can is large and a small tube). Each manufacturer has its recommendations, read the instructions.

Do not measure by eye!

The base and catalyst have different densities and therefore require thorough mixing. Stir for at least 2 minutes. You can whip with a mixer at low speed! At high speeds, the mass quickly solidifies.

The shape of the product, which you will re-create, it is better to grease with Johnsons Baby oil- Can be replaced with petroleum jelly.

Then you fill in the form that you want to repeat. Withstand the time, according to the manufacturer's recommendations, and your mold is ready.

The temperature of the room and the compound must be at least 20 degrees.

The market praises the American smooth - on silicone, the Alcorplast company (vk.com/alcorplast). There are also Russian brands, for example, "Zaitsevskie silicones" (elastoform24.ru) or "Penta" (itwpenta.ru).

If you choose Molds ready to pay attention to the Molds, which form inside the glossy surface. This will save you time and wasted resin.

15. GOMMA IN PASTA

Cool stuff from @resinpro.ru @resinpro.it GOMMA IN PASTA is non-toxic silicone rubber. With paste, you can make molds in minutes at home.

Two-component paste, mixed in equal proportions 1: 1 until a homogeneous mixture is obtained.

You pinch off one component A and component B in equal proportions, mix everything until a homogeneous mixture (stir for 2-3 minutes) and after about 25-35 minutes the paste takes the form that you intended to make. Use the basis for pasty silicone heavy Tel'nykh Plexiglas or dense film (white greenhouse can be used).

For 1 mold of a cup holder (medium size, 9-11 cm), the consumption of silicone rubber is 40-50 g of total mass (A + B). The cans are enough for about 10-11 molds, 45-50 grams each.

You just have to press down on top of the paste model MDL which we are doing and wait for the complete drying. Once dry, you can pour in the resin.

Do not use at temperatures below 8-10 ° C.

Pros:
•non-toxic silicone rubber.
•get the form we need quickly.
•fast solidification of compounds.

Contras:
•price.
• formation of holes on silicone. When cast with resin, a non-smooth surface is formed. Requires finishing for the gloss of the product from the back.

16. BEAUTIFUL SIDES (ENDS) OF THE PICTURE

There are a few tips you can use to keep your bumpers beautiful.

• you can paint the sides with regular acrylic paint.

• sides can be covered with gold (bronze, gold, silver).

• they also can be decorated with textured paste. Craquelure, for example.

• you can also make your bumpers a continuation of the painting.

For this:

1. You can use sandpaper for the edges of the base, remove the sharp edge as if rounding it. This is to ensure that the resin can drain well.

2. Prime the sides with acrylic in the color that will cover the entire base. Wait until it is completely dry.

3. Stick the tape around the picture.

4. Add + 10-15% resin to the total resin on your bumpers.

5. Fill the picture according to your idea.

6. Then wait for your resin to take its density on the finished job to remove the tape from the sides.

Approximately 20-25 minutes after work, depending on the resin manufacturer, room temperature, and viscosity, you will see the condition of the resin.

The resin should be as thick as honey or thick caramel. Move the scotch tape a little - the side, see the consistency of the resin.

If the resin becomes like caramel, it will slowly and beautiful envelop your sides of the tablet, repeating the pattern. Now it's time to remove our scotch tape.

After 10 minutes, go to the picture and use a spatula to collect the dripped droplets from the bottom, so that after drying, the adhesive tape can easily come off the back surface.

Professional tablets already have beveled edges.

17. REMOVING OF THE MASKING TAPE

The next day, as the resin has dried, you have some resin beads on the back of the painting. The droplets easily come off along with the masking tape by heating with a hairdryer.

The dryer can hold obliquely, blowing out under the masking tape, and pull in the direction of the scotch tape, it will be removed soon. You can help with a stationery knife.

If cured resin remains on some areas of the tablets, remove it with a grinding machine or encryption paper.

 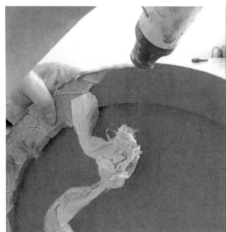 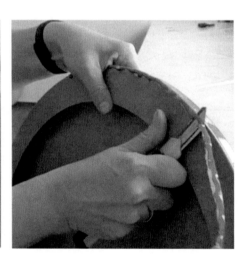

18. EPOXY REMOVING

How to remove epoxy resin from hand skin?

Fresh epoxy can be cleaned easily with Pampers baby wipes (they have a higher alcohol content than other brands). If the epoxy has hardened on the skin, moisten a tissue with 3% vinegar and rub gently into the skin until the epoxy is soft so that it can easily peel off.

You can also use nail polish remover or thinner (has a strong odor). After that, wash your hands with soap and apply a cream to the affected area of the skin to soothe the skin.

How to remove epoxy from clothing and fabrics?

It is necessary to lower the cloth into a container of boiling water for a few seconds, then remove the softened resin. Next, wash clothes with regular detergent.

In tissues that do not withstand heating, apply 3% vinegar, to soften the resin and remove excess faded portion in cool water.

How to remove epoxy from plastic or glass?

Any solvent, isopropyl alcohol, regular scraper, or spatula can help. After removing the resin, wipe the surface with a damp cloth.

How to remove epoxy from the floor?

If you have tiles, laminate, or parquet on your floor, then it can be perfectly cleaned with a scraper or trowel. If it doesn't clean, heat it a little with a hairdryer and a scraper will help you.

Carpet - you cannot remove the hardened resin from it with anything. You only have to throw it away.

19. MOUNTS FOR PICTURES

There are a lot of fasteners on the market. Each painting has its fasteners, consider the weight of the painting, the wall you will hang on, the frame, and the choice is yours.

Details for fasteners can be different: chains, cords, glue, buttons, nails.

How the paintings are attached:

• If the paintings are small, they can be glued onto foam double-sided tape. Convenient in that you do not need to drill. But there is a risk of tearing off the plaster along with the tape when transferring the picture. Before peeling off, direct a stream of a hot hairdryer to soften the tape.

• Velcro from Command 3M. Suitable for all walls and can withstand paintings up to 7kg. Do not forget to degrease the place you will be gluing.

• Crocodile pendant. Also used for wall hanging.

• If the picture is large, then you can make a suspension in the form of a nylon cable.

• If the picture is very difficult, then mounts for mirrors will help you out.

• You can glue them on the back of the painting with epoxy. For particularly heavy paintings, an expansion anchor can be used. This tube length of 5 cm the entire length of which passes a bolt ending head screwdriver, nut or hook.

• Self-tapping screws are easily screwed into a drywall sheet, nails are driven in, but the material itself is fragile and holds this type of fastener unreliably. Special hooks with nails made of extra strong metal. Regular nails simply bend when trying to hammer into a wall. As an alternative, hardware stores offer special designs - hooks made of plastic, into which nails from hardened metal are soldered. They are driven into any wall with an ordinary hammer.

 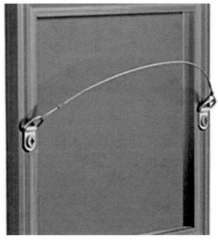 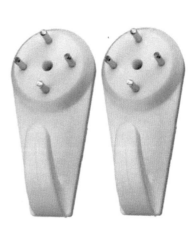

20. VISUALIZATION OF PAINTINGS

Visualization is important for a person, because our attention is focused on the result, as a result of which there is an impact on the subconscious, and this is the connecting thread of the fulfillment of desire. Therefore, visualization is necessary for the successful sale of your products and paintings.

For the successful sale of your paintings, you need high-quality photographs in interiors.

To create the visualization, we use the following programs:

• Adobe Photoshop is a multifunctional program in which you can insert a picture of a ready-made interior layout. The pictures are more realistic since a falling shadow can be applied to it.

• Canva.com is an online service that allows you to do anything with ready-made or imaginary templates, I am very happy with it. There you can also visualize your paintings in the interior. Unfortunately, the drop shadow in the Canva has not yet been invented.

• PhotoLayers is a phone app. For those who cannot work on a PC and need to quickly render, this application will suit you. It's free and easy to use. Download the mockup to your phone and insert your picture.

There are a huge number of applications and programs for visualizing paintings/products. I told you about my methods, perhaps you will choose others for yourself.

You can download interiors for your paintings (mockups) for free. In the search, type "interior mockups", download for free the interior that suits your picture, and use the applications that I wrote above, inserting your picture into the mockup.

A useful site for visualization is www.airbnb.ru. There are many interiors for every taste from all countries. This will help the customer understand how the picture being tried on will look in a normal interior.

21. RESIN PAINTINGS CARE

Each item loses its original properties over time, losing its initial attractiveness. Resin paintings are no exception.

The following rules must be remembered so that the resin painting will please you for a long time:
• In the first 5-7 days, remove the painting from direct sunlight, so it will retain the colors longer and will not turn yellow.
• Do not hang the painting overheating appliances or in direct sunlight. The resin composition does not tolerate long-term high-temperature exposure. The resin may turn yellow faster.
• Resin products cured under the influence of alcohol can soften and cloud the surface. Therefore, it is not necessary to wipe the work with any alcohol, except for a glass cleaner. If necessary, a glass cleaner can be applied to the picture after complete drying, preferably after 2 days.
• You can wipe your product with laminated clothes, woolen, or flannel.
• Products with resin are also afraid of water. If you wipe the resin product with water, be sure to wipe the product dry. Water droplets create stains that are difficult to get rid of afterward.
• Resin products tend to break if made without a backing. Do not drop.
• It is best to store resin bijouterie in a dark, dry place so that the plants inside the product do not fade and are less scratched themselves.

In the first days after pouring, if the product is accidentally scratched, it can be corrected by heating the damaged area with a hairdryer. Then rub on top with a cloth for laminated surfaces. So your defect will go away without a trace and you won't have to fill it.

Heat absent-mindedly, not pointwise, to avoid yellowing or damaging the resin.

To make your picture harmoniously fit into the interior, choose an interior that is similar in color to your painting, at least one element that repeats the color.

22. PREPARATORY STAGE

The preparatory stage for working with epoxy will almost always be the same.

1. We prepare our work surface by covering it with a film.

2. We take our tablet

3. With the level we define our slope of the surface, we level it so that the resin does not flow down to one edge. If you don't have a level, you can use the Surface Level application on your phone.

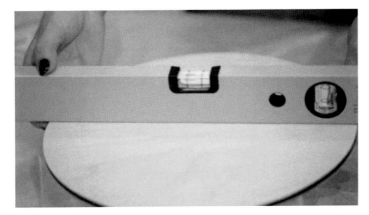

4. We prime the tablet with primer or acrylic paints. (see. in the section "Primer for bases "). Don't forget to prime the bumpers! We are waiting for complete drying.

5. We glue the back surface of the tablet with masking tape and make the sides if you wish. Press the tape firmly against the sides of the tablet. This will help control our resin. We can also protect the back surface of the work from drops of resin with reinforced tape.

6. We put our tablet on the cups, and if you have a canvas, put it on a stretcher.

7. We put on nitrile gloves, and preferably two gloves at once. Some got dirty, we shoot, the second is already on hand.

 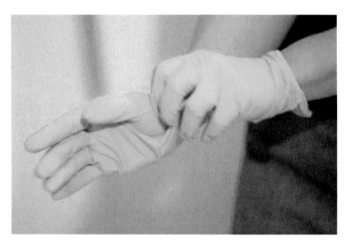

8. We decide on our drawing. You can first sketch with a pencil on paper the approximate movement of the resin.

9. We select colors for our drawing.

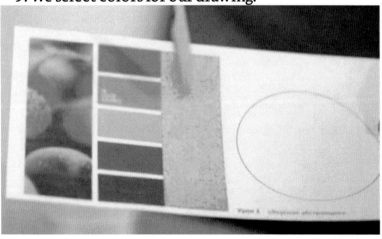 

10. We calculate the amount of resin for our area. Remember the formula X * Y * 1.2 (1.3) = the

amount of resin

where X = layer thickness in mm, Y = area in m2 (see details in the section 7. Resin consumption). If the sides of your tablet/canvas are high, you will need to add 0.5% of the total resin to the sides.

11. We take the scales. To prevent the scales from getting dirty, you can wrap them with cling film.

12. We prepare a large container for mixing the resin.

13. We put on a respirator (for details, see the section "SAFETY").

14. We measure out the required proportions of resin, in our case, it is 2: 1 - 2 parts of resin (A) and 1 part of hardener (B). Check with the resin manufacturer.

15. We mix the resin with the hardener. Mix thoroughly with a wooden stick/spatula for 4-5 minutes in a glass. When mixing, do not forget to scrape off the resin from the walls of the container. This must be done for a homogeneous mass so that there is no sticky layer on the product after drying.

Do not forget that under normal working conditions (temperature and humidity in the room), the working time with the resin is from 30 to 45 minutes (depending on the manufacturer of the resin), read on the label of the purchased resin. There is a resin that is active for 15 to 25 minutes.

16. We take a certain number of cups, according to our idea.

17. Pour resin into cups in the correct proportions. Usually, less resin should be left on metallics (gold, silver, bronze).

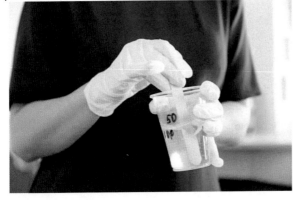 

18. Mix dyes into each cup (no more than 5-7% of the volume), mix for about 5-10 seconds und, bring to a homogeneous mass with epoxy resin. We determine the brightness, color density ourselves, according to our idea.

19. We pour each color onto a tablet/canvas, according to our idea.

20. Blow with a hairdryer / move the tablet from side to side.

21. If necessary, use a burner to expel bubbles from our picture. If you accidentally ruin a part of the product with a burner, try to remove the part of the spoiled resin and refill. If the resin is already half-hardened, and you ruined your plan, wait until the resin has completely dried, sand the damaged area, and then pour it over again with transparent resin.

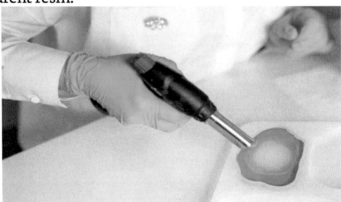

22. Wait about 20-30 minutes, when the resin becomes viscous, like honey or like thick caramel.

23. We carefully remove our sides from the tape so that the resin flows beautifully and envelops our edges. With such bumpers, there will be a continuation of the picture.

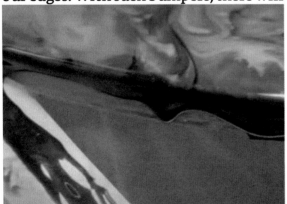

24. After about 5 minutes, remove the excess droplets of flowing resin with a spatula from the bottom of the tablet.

25. We cover our tablet/canvas with a protective film from dust. With a stick/awl/toothpick, you can remove dust particles from the picture.

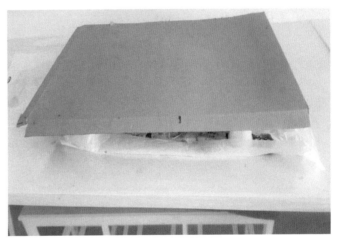

26. We are waiting for the resin to dry completely. Curing time 24 hours, resin fully cured after 72 hours.

27. Remove the tape from the back of the tablet/canvas. (see the section 17. Removing of the masking tape section).

28. If necessary, we grind the back surface of the painting either with a grinder or manually with sandpaper. Grit sandpaper for the final takes 63-80 (P-180 labeling).

29. We enjoy our masterpiece.

23. LESSON 1 "DELICIOUS ABSTRACTION"

To create the painting "Abstraction" first read the section 22. Preparatory stage.
I will highlight the main points to pay attention to.

1. Don't forget about the beautiful borders of your picture.

2. If this is not a professional tablet, remember that you can independently sandpaper the edges of the tree, remove the sharp edge so that the resin flows better, and envelops the edges of the picture.

3. Don't forget about the safety precautions!

4. In step 10, you need to calculate the amount of resin for our area. Remember the formula $X * Y * 1.2 (1.3)$ = amount of resin, where X = layer thickness in mm, Y = area in m2 (for more details, see the section 7. Resin consumption).

Example 1:

If your sides are 1-2mm, take a factor of 1.2.

For example, we have a tablet with a diameter of 40cm. We want to fill our painting with a thickness of 1mm. Bumpers 3mm.

$1 * 0.40 * 1.2 = 0.48 * 1000 = 480$ grams of resin we need for our painting.

Component A (resin) = 320 g

Component B (hardener) = 160 g

Example 2:

If your sides are 3-5mm, use a factor of 1.3 instead of 1.2. For example, we have a tablet with a diameter of 40cm. We want to fill our painting with a thickness of 1mm. Bumpers 1cm.

$1 * 0.40 * 1.3 = 0.52 * 1000 = 520$ grams of resin we need for our painting.

Component A (resin) = 347 g

Component B (hardener) = 173 g

5. When mixing dye or pigments, your color will be different from the color in the cup when you pour it onto a wooden tablet.

The color on the glass is always much darker than on the picture. Therefore, I recommend looking at the spatula, you can see what color you will have on the tablet.

Pastel colors are obtained by adding half a drop of dye to already white color and so bring it to the shade you need.

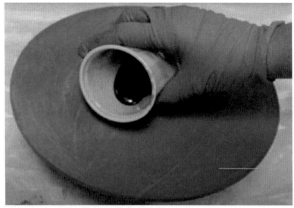

6. We begin to form our drawing, pouring alternately colors onto the tablet in a chaotic manner. You can move the layers of painted resin by tilting the picture in different directions, using sticks to form the final pattern. You can also roll out the resin with a hairdryer, connecting the colors, but not too much so that there is no dirt.

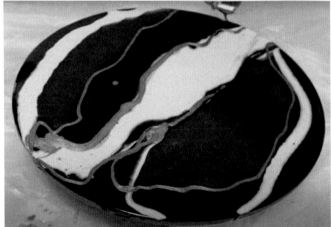

7. The easiest way to remove bubbles is to locally heat, either with a technical hairdryer or with a burner, those places where there are accumulations near the surface. If you use a burner, you need to lightly touch the surface, drive in different directions, if the resin boils, the picture will be damaged.

8. When you've got the drawing you want, cover your work with dust.

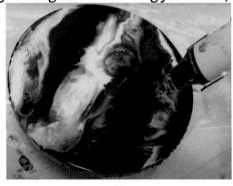

Remember, the less you climb to the resin, the more interesting the drawing, turn off your perfectionism, surrender to the flow, and enjoy.

24. LESSON 2 "AUSTRALIAN AND CLASSIC SEAS"

Marine style is the choice of romantic natures who expect inspiration and an atmosphere of freedom from the interior. The variety of marine shades is amazing.

The process of working with epoxy resin is the same as in section 22. Preparatory stage, just follow everything in stages. You will need a liquid or medium viscosity resin.

I will highlight the main points, what to look for:

1. We prime the tablet with acrylic paints, making a stretch from the darkest to the lightest. You can skip the gradient between colors, leaving your surface pure white, but if you want to express the depth of your painting, I recommend using acrylic paint for smooth transitions.

The underpainting can be applied with a foam roller or soft brushes to avoid streaking.

2. Pour resin into cups in the right proportions, according to our idea. We leave the least amount of resin on the waves.

3. Add sand to the first glass of resin. We pour so much sand that it is not very thick.

4. Mix RESI Wave/Wave effect/Cell effect into a smaller glass. Add a little bit to create a wave

effect. When adding a large amount of powder may cause sediment in the picture, so mix it thoroughly (about 2 minutes).

5. Start pouring the resin onto the tablet from above and walk towards the shore - from dark to light (shore).

6. Spread the resin with your hands, a spatula, or a palette knife, combining the shades of resin so that the transitions are not so sharp, but light.

A technical hairdryer can then warm up the resin if it is difficult to spread with your hands.

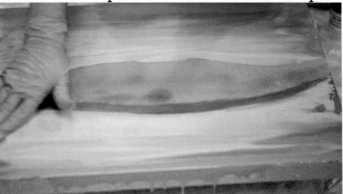

7. To reduce the resin slipping to the shore, start blowing it up from the shore. If you need to move the color up / down, just tilt your tablet a little in the direction you need.

8. Then apply the Resi Wave foam in waves. Make a spout by the cup and starting from the edge, pour out the waves.

Liquid resin is used to obtain large cells in waves!

Resi Blast (Cell Creation Additive) will leave craters! in your painting that can only be gotten rid of by refilling.

9. Heat these waves from above with a hairdryer. You can walk with a burner. Leave it for 1 minute for the openwork to appear on our waves.

10. The powder starts to work like that.Then start creating your waves by rolling them out with a hairdryer. It is necessary to inflate the waves tangentially to the plane of the picture as if pushing onto the shore. Your task is to create a beautiful wave to make the waves appear realistic.

The hairdryer can be switched to medium power for easier control over the direction of the wave. You can correct the waves with a palette knife or a wooden stick.

11. If you wish, you can decorate your shore with moss-stabilized shells. After complete drying, you can paint with acrylic turtles, footprints in the sand, fish, whatever. After that, fill it with transparent resin again and make waves for a volumetric effect.

12. After 40-45 minutes, remove the sides so that your thick caramel resin flows down, enveloping the edges of the painting beautifully.

13. Remember that the less we interfere in the process, the more grateful the resin is. Enjoy the process.

The seas can be of different shades, see the section 39. "Picture set for inspiration".

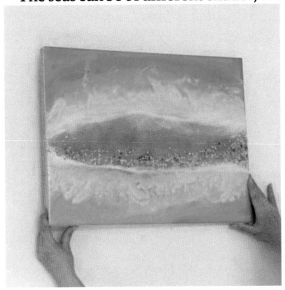

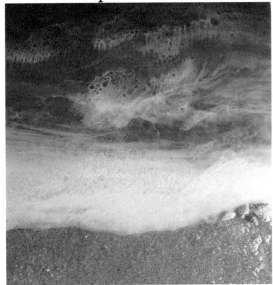

25. LESSON 3 "GEODE"

Geode is a natural mineral. The shape of the geode can be any, but more often it is isometric, round.

I'll tell you how to create an imitation of a geode cut by yourself using epoxy resin. To do this, prepare sparkles, glass chips to create a natural stone; hot gun, liquid potal, texture paste, and the very form-based for Geode. You can cut the base yourself with a jigsaw and MDF.

There can be different stone shapes: square, round, with curved lines in the form of a stone, in the middle of the tablet there is a hole (see the section 40. Photo selection).

Principle of creating a geode

1. Think over the drawing of your Geode in advance. Draw on paper or on the board itself, where you will have lines, where the stones will be located, what color scheme.

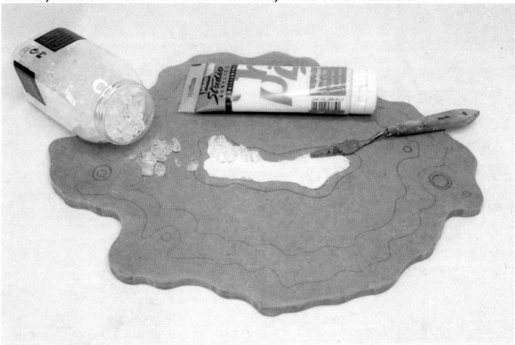

2. Place masking tape on the back of the tablet.
3. Prime the entire tablet with acrylic paint according to your idea. When choosing colors, it is desirable to have 1 contrasting color (so that the composition does not merge) +, if desired, gold/silver/copper.

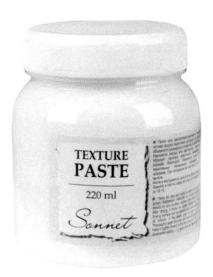

4. Create a rough edge of the stone.

Apply a layer of any texture paste (Sonnet paste) inside the Geode hole and optionally around the edges 3-4 cm in width. Sprinkle natural stones/glass chips on top of the paste or glue with a hot pistol. A hot gun will take longer than pasta.

It is easier to sprinkle the stones with a spoon. The process will take twice as long as with decorative paste. As you stir the resin, your paste will harden. Create an imitation of a cut of the mineral.

5. Along the edge of the tablet, you can make a side - a strip with hot glue, then paint it with gold / silver liquid gold leaf. You can do it without aside, as you like.

6. You can start pouring resin both from the edge of the Geode and from the center in different colors, according to your idea, in straight or winding lines, mixing a little with a bright accent and gold/silver/copper. You can roll out the drawing with a hairdryer, but do not overdo it, remember, the less we climb to the resin, the more grateful it is to us.

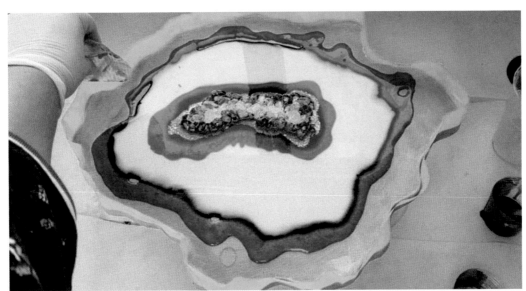

7. The next day, you can use a glass marker to draw lines across the entire surface of your Geode. To do this, you can see a photo of these Geodes in "photo selection" so you can repeat the cutoff line for naturalness.

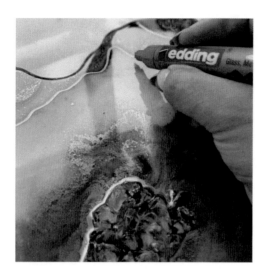 

8. If desired, you can fill in the second layer with accents - thin stripes (sparkles, gold, silver, copper).

9. The edge of the Geode can also be painted with liquid gold, gold/silver paint if you do not have a continuation of the drawing on the tablet.

10. After drawing the lines, on top of the dried resin, apply a second coat of clear resin for the depth of the drawing.

Glass chips for your painting can be painted in the color you want in two ways:

Pour the required amount of stones/glass into a separate glass and add alcohol ink of the color you need there. Cover with a glove and shake until mixed.

Pour a little resin into a separate glass and add the pigment you want to color the stones with. Stir with a spoon. Stones/glass must not float in resin!

26. LESSON 4 "MARBLE"

Marble is a unique natural stone, rock. There are different colors (see the section 40. Photo selection).

This natural material can also be created using epoxy.

Shape of marble

You can imitate marble on almost any surface that can be painted. Paintings look better - marble with right angles, not round.

Marble color

If you want to repeat the natural motives of the stone (marble), you need to observe moderation in colors. Active colored marble is good for laconic interiors. Reproduce the similarity of marble using natural colors. Remember that one color should always be an accent in our works. Select three different shades, which create your "marble" pattern. Choose the fourth color to simulate veins.

Principle of operation

1. We do all the steps as in the "Preparatory stage" section.

2. When pouring our resin into cups, we make sure to leave resin for bronze/gold/silver, according to your drawing and idea of marble.

3. Spread the resin with the base color all over the tablet (for example, it's white). In white, you can add Cobalt pearlescent pigment for the effect and depth of the marble.

4. You can spread the resin either with a palette knife or with a gloved hand. Carefully remove the upper gloves, you have a second pair on your hands.

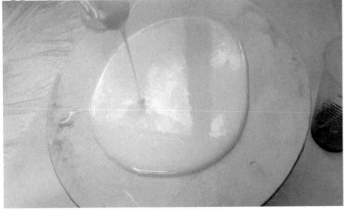 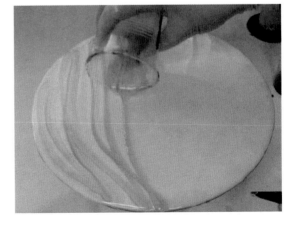

5. Take the first resin color and start to create thin lines of marble veins (eg bronze) with lines.

6. In the main color of marble (white, beige, pearl, etc.) add 2-3 there drops of beige pigment + bronze (you can add alcohol ink).　　6. In the main color of marble (white, beige, pearl, etc.) add 2-3 there drops of beige pigment + bronze (you can add alcohol ink).

One Glass Technique

Then, without stirring, pour this mixture in strips onto your tablet. This will create natural veins that imitate real marble. You can roll your veins a little with a palette knife on the tablet. Your lines don't have to be straight.

 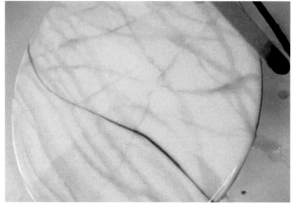

7. With a dark color, we draw lines with a stick that looks like slingshots, creating an imitation of a stone.

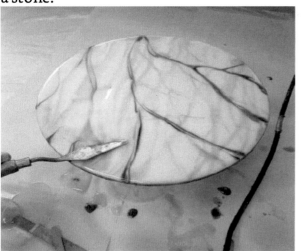 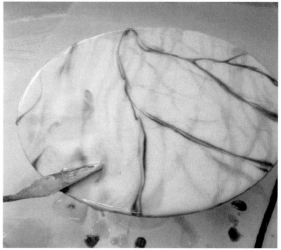

8. With a hairdryer, neatly at a right angle, you can slightly inflate the veins without disturbing the structure of the pattern.

  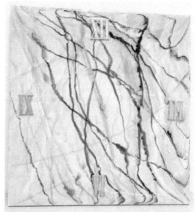

In a cold room, the cure rate of the resin decreases.

27. LESSON 5 "CLOCK WITH STONES"

With epoxy resin, you can create any clock as a decoration. You will need:
• round/square/rectangular tablet with a hole in the middle,
• resin of any viscosity,
• pigments, stones
• mechanism + arrows.

Any work should start with drawing on paper so that there is no spoiled resin and upset feelings. Lay out the composition on your watch for clarity.

If you have an idea to make stones around the edges of the clock, but also think over the details (the color of the stones in what color), whether you will have a dial, numbers or will there be a watch without anything but hands.

You can use a cocktail tube or rolled paper to secure the center of the watch so that the resin does not flood the hole for the watch movement.

1. We do all the stages as described in the "Preparatory Stage" section.

2. Fill your watch with resin according to your drawing (green, blue, gold, and some white). It could be the dirty glass technique, it could be lined, marbled, or just a tone without a pattern.

3. Take into account the thickness of the fill and the height of the stones, as this influences the choice of the height of the movement!

4. After 20-25 minutes, when the resin has set a little, you can put on top of the clock dial/numbers/divisions. If you put the numbers ahead of time, they will immediately drown in the resin.

Dial/numbers/graduations you can paint with acrylic paint, cover spray paint, or gold leaf (gold/silver/bronze). Can be laser engraved dial/graduation/numbers from the mirror.

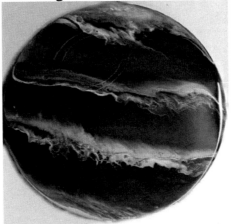

5. If you want to use stones along the rim of your tablet, mix stones/glass with a little clear resin. Stir so that the resin only slightly envelops your stones/glass and spread them gently with a spoon in a circle.

6. The top can be lightly poured over your stones/glass chips with a clear resin to secure.

7. The arrows can be painted with anything: spray varnish (there is a varnish as shiny as glass), covered with gold leaf or nail varnish of the desired color.

8. After complete drying, we remove the tube (or cardboard paper from the center, helping with a hairdryer, if it does not come off the resin badly), insert the clock mechanism and hands.

Dirty glass technique: pour all mixed resin shades or some part of it into one glass. After turning the glass over the tablet and wait for the resin to drain (20 seconds). With this method, cells are usually formed.

The dial can be ordered from laser cutters. The dial thickness must be at least 2mm, otherwise, it will sink in the resin. It can be either wooden or mirrored. The wooden dial is covered with gold leaf, painted with any acrylic paint, or covered with spray paint.

28. LESSON 6 "ART IN PETRI CUPS"

Petri is a mesmerizing technique for creating a micro-universe using epoxy resin and alcohol ink.

The German bacteriologist Julius Petri created a universe of bacteria in such a cup, filling it with substances for microorganisms. The Petri Cup was named after him.

The founders of the Petry Art technique are considered to be two artists Josie Lewis and Clary Reis, who of them was the first to turn it into art - opinions still differ. In this technique, you can make paintings, coasters, boxes, jewelry.

How are such intricate beautiful patterns created?

You will need:
• resin (medium viscosity),
• Alcohol ink (preferably refills), Mixative white ink, Ranger TAL31611 Adirondack,
• any silicone molds.

Work order

1. Liquid resin is not used in this technique, since the white ink dye will all fall to the bottom and harden with ugly white blots, and in the thick resin, your dye will not penetrate as it should, almost all of it will remain on the surface. Therefore, a medium viscosity resin is ideal.

2. Pour the prepared resin already mixed in the cup into the silicone mold. Heat the resin with a small burner in quick strokes. Wait 10 minutes.

3. Prepare the colors of alcohol ink you want to use + white Mixative ink (they are perfect for Petri).

4. Start to drip over the entire surface in the silicone mold a single ink color and then on top of that color drip white ink Mixative and so alternately 4-5 times, depending on the volume of Mold dripping ink + white ink (a drop of color + drop white). During this time, the ink interacts with the epoxy and creates streaks that look like bacteria. White ink is heavier, so it sinks to the bottom, creating an unusual effect. The drop should diverge slowly!

5. Once you're done, cover your silicone mold with dust.

6. After completely curing, remove your masterpiece from the silicone mold carefully, starting from the sides.

Know how to stop in time to make the drawing effective and unusual. If you drip a lot of white Mixative, there may be drops, as this ink is heavier than usual.

Debris from silicone molds can be removed with clear tape. All dust particles and pellets from previous fillings perfectly remain on it. Molds are washed in soapy water, then rinsed and wiped dry, stored in a bag to protect from dust and other damage.

Petri can be of different diameters, they can be placed on stands, decorating your space.

29. LESSON 7 "BIJOUTERIE FROM JEWELRY RESIN".

Epoxy resin bijouterie is gaining popularity. They are bright, original, and will give your image an unusual charm. Necklace, pendants, rings, resin earrings are a wonderful gift for yourself and your friends.

In this case, I recommend taking a proven jewelry resin for jewelry, which will not turn yellow soon. This resin is a little more expensive than regular creative resin.

Your products can be supplemented with:
• dried flowers (live plants will rot in resin, turn into a black mass),
  • stones (glass chips of the fine fraction),
  • metal elements (for example, steampunk style),
  • rhinestones, sequins,
  • alcohol ink,
  • potal,
  • wood (can be charred or ordinary),
  • stabilized moss,
  • phosphor,
  • holographic stickers, etc.

Work order:

1. Prepare your workplace.
2. Prepare your Molds for jewelry.
3. Mix resin for jewelry. Start injecting the hardener slowly so that no bubbles form. The resin is mixed for about 10 minutes. Let the resin sit for 30 minutes.
4. Pour the resulting mixture into another cup, so as not to remain the particles unmixed resin.
5. Place the decorative elements in the silicone mold according to your drawing.
6. Pour in a thin stream of resin, starting at the edge.
7. Protect your mold from dust.
8. After complete curing, carefully remove your product from the mold.
9. If the excess resin has formed, cut it off with scissors or tweezers until the resin is plastic. Edges that have been cut can be polished with a file/trowel / fine sandpaper.

Larger products are first sanded with a coarse abrasive, bringing to transparency (for polishing products, see below in this section).

You can also try a different fill method. To do this, pour a little resin into the silicone mold and let it dry completely. The next day, without getting the resin out of the mold, start laying out your composition, distributing the decorative elements with tweezers or a toothpick. Then fill it again with clear resin until the end.

If you are pouring a hemisphere, then I recommend pouring it just above the mold, since the flat part of the hemisphere will have to be sanded. After a day, or maybe more, take out your product carefully.

After that accessories are added and your product is ready.

If your cabochon (molds for jewelry) is small, you can use a syringe for filling. It's convenient, and you won't spill too much.

Before buying accessories, consider the future image of the product. Buy only from trusted online creative stores where all products are of high quality. This is a guarantee that the epoxy product you create will look beautiful and will last for many years, and if you work on the order, you will have confidence in your product.

It is important that the surface is level and does not tilt. After you fill in the lens, it is best not to move your jewelry until it is frozen, as the resin will leak out and disrupt your composition.

Epoxy resin jewelry fittings

Fittings are an important connecting link on which your product will look expensive or cheap and how long it will serve you or your customer.

• Settings are the base for resin jewelry. Blanks come in the form of frames with borders for pouring. The fittings are completely ready for use and work, it is only necessary to fill the base with an epoxy resin casting.

There are settings: for earrings, pendants, rings, hairpins, and brooches. There are different forms. The material can be stainless steel, iron, brass, or zinc alloy.

• Bales are unusual holders on which a necklace or pendant is put on. Bale is a figured ring with a loop for attaching additional accessories to the base of the jewelry.

• Laces, chains for pendants. There are different types (from suede, silver, gold, brass, leather, waxed with a lock, plastic-textile, fabric, velvet, nylon, etc.), which can be purchased on the Internet.

The fittings are attached in different ways. In the finished resin product, you can carefully drill a hole with a Dremel or awl. You can screw the channel into your frozen product, fix it on top with glue for strength.

All super glues are afraid of exposure to sweat and do not like the sun's rays of cold. Therefore, I recommend E6000 industrial adhesive. It is ideal for gluing fittings. There is a special set of tools for making jewelry: round-nose pliers, wire cutters, pliers. They are necessary to hold everything together beautifully.

  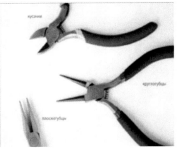 

To achieve a shiny surface of the product, you should choose molds with glossy walls. The matte base of the molds will give the same "look" to the epoxy decorations.

Polishing products

After the product has completely dried, additional correction is required.

1. Dremel (with a milling cutter or a manicure machine or by hand) go through the dirty stage of cleaning irregularities with an abrasive with a coarse degree of roughness. Initial buffing will remove the unevenness, leaving your garment smooth. Do not forget to wear a respirator to prevent small particles from entering the respiratory tract.

2. The decoration is given transparency. To do this, it is necessary to start with a coarse abrasive, then gradually lower the grain size, bringing the object to a perfectly even state.

You need to start with sandpaper 600, then 800, then 1200 and 2500. Constantly wetting the product a little in water. Paper grain is shown on the back of P100, P600, P1200, etc.

You can polish by hand (longer) or with a Dremel. Tips on Dremel can be purchased as in the picture, with different circles of grain. Don't forget the paste polishing roller.

After all, this, use a foam pad with goi paste (green or gray polishing paste) or any other polishing paste, bring to a shine, also with water. On the roller, apply a little paste (it is very economical) and rub MANUAL in the product, and then turn the Dremel. Otherwise, everything will be in paste).

In addition to GOI paste, 3M car polishing pastes are suitable. In Russia, they praise the MIRKA polishing paste, write about it, which creates a mirror shine. I haven't tried it myself, I have GOI pasta brought from Russia.

Polishes containing silicone add shine to the product, but the effect disappears quickly after damp cloth.

Before polishing, it is necessary to remove dust from the surface of the product, otherwise, perfect polishing cannot be achieved.

30. LESSON 8 "COSMOS"

Pictures of space always attract people, because the world is so boundless, mysterious, and alluring. And you can create your own space using epoxy.

You will need:
- round tablet (canvas) of any diameter,
- medium viscosity resin,
- pigments, glass markers.

Work order:

1. We do all the stages as described in the "Preparatory Stage" section.

2. We paint the base with dark acrylic paint (it can be a deep dark blue, dark purple, black). Do not forget about the sides, paint them in a dark color too.

 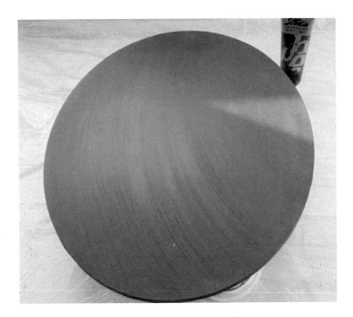

3. Next, the stars are drawn on our tablet. Take a hard bristle brush, dip it in white acrylic paint and start splattering to create our stars. After that, you can drag your hand once (in the center, for example) to the side over the white paint, this will create the effect of flares and galaxies. Space will become more alive.

4. Wait until the tablet is completely dry.

5. Check the working surface with a level so that there are no distortions.

6. Decide on the colors of the cosmos. Usually, these are orange, purple, blue, a little yellow (beige), red. Don't forget white too.

7. Mix resin (any viscosity) according to the rules and divide it into two cups of resin.

8. In the first cup of clear resin, add glitter to a blue or purple resin. Your drawing will begin to shimmer.

9. Fill the entire surface with this shiny-transparent resin. You can spread and stretch the resin by hand.

10. Run a burner over the flickering resin.

11. Divide the second glass of clear resin into colors, tint them.

12. Start pouring the lines of your space, without a special pattern, after blowing a hairdryer, start rolling out the resin.

13. With white/beige, you can make the nebula a sinuous line.

14. With a hairdryer, draw our planets and flares. You can create these planets with drops of resin of different diameters.

15. After drying, you can draw a couple of inclusions of stars with a marker on the glass. Top with clear resin with blue sparkles (optional).

31. LESSON 9 " HOLDERS FOR VARIOUS STUFF "

What are resin holders for, how to use them:
• for table setting
• for decoration
• under soap
• under the candles
• under perfume
• for decorative elements.

Stands come in completely different shapes: round, square, triangular, hexagonal, flower-shaped, geode-shaped, wing-shaped, pomegranate-shaped, etc.
Holders molds are on sale (Instagram, AliExpress, Etsy, online stores that deal with resin).

You can create your unique stuff- holders with:
• non-toxic rubber Gomma in Pasta (see the section above about rubber) or silicone.
• injection molding silicone, create your mold (wings, pomegranate, apple, strawberry, etc.).
You can make a blank for your shape yourself.

First Way

1. Draw on paper or download a picture you like, give it to laser cutting from plywood 3-4 mm.

2. Prepare your work surface. It can be dense glossy white film, film for lamination, plexiglass 4-5mm thick! Thin plexiglass bends from the temperature of the resin and it will be more difficult to snap off finished products.

3. Place your stuff- holder on the table.

4. Take Gomma paste and mix according to the instructions.

5. Create edges with ready-made pasty silicone around your wood by pressing the paste firmly against the plexiglass (film) this mixture. You have up to 10 minutes for this, the paste gradually begins to freeze, have time. Smooth out the silicone with gloves and soapy water.

6. Leave on for 25-35 minutes until the rubber is completely cured. Such a mold does not wear out like a simple silicone one, it is considered reusable. Silicone hardened form from the paste easily departs from the solidified resin. Re- mold can be used many times, adheres to other surfaces perfectly.

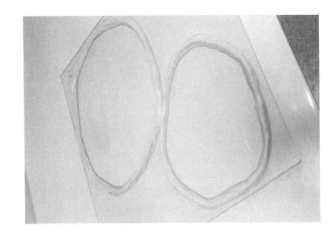

Second way

1. You will need 4-5mm plexiglass and silicone sealant.

2. Draw a free-form pattern on the plexiglass.

3. With sealant, trace along the drawn path, creating a shape. Squeeze out another strip of sealant on top of the first coat.

4. With gloves and a soapy solution, run your fingers along the inner edge, leveling the sealant so that your cup holder edge is smooth.

5. Wait for the sealant to harden.

6. You can use such a mold two or three times so that there are no scratches on the backside (on the plexiglass). But you can always fill in scratches with a thin layer of resin.

There are principles you should understand when experimenting with stiff-holders:
- The resin always flows down to the center of the mold,
- The pattern of the cup holders depends on the viscosity of the resin,
- Bubbles can always be removed with a burner,
- A finishing layer is required for stuff-holders (thermal protection or just finish).
- There are many ways to create beautiful resin designs.

I'll show you a few options.

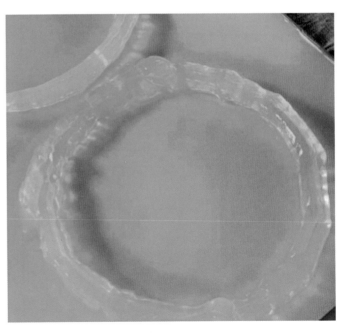

Before   After

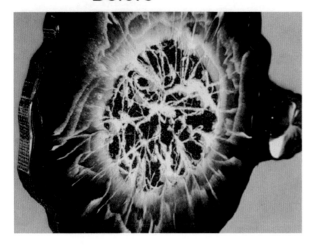

Coasters with liquid resin. Technology "Veil"

Approximate consumption of resin for 1 holder with a diameter of 9-12cm = 80-85 g of resin. For example, 4 stuff-holders will require 320 g of liquid resin, including 107 g of hardener (B) and 213 g of resin (A).

Work order:

1. Pour the resin into three cups. Mix in them:
• any dark color 5 drops,
• any color is a transparent toner, make the shade lighter than the first.
• gold / sequins
• leave the most transparent resin, about 45-50% of the total
2. After mixing the pigments with the resin, do not wait, start pouring immediately.
3. Pour a thin layer of dark-colored resin around the edge of the stuff-holder.
4. Then make a second layer of clear toner.
5. Pour in clear resin over the first two layers of resin.
6. Pour clear gold/glitter resin into the center of the stuff-holder.

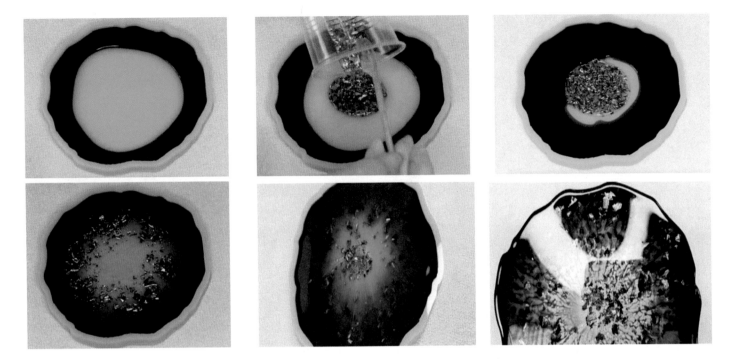

7. The resin tends to the center of the mold, and your dark resin color will also tend to the center, forming lines that drift towards the very center.

8. Go through the burner to remove bubbles.

9. Cover the holder from the dust, and try not to touch it(not with a burner , do not move, nothing).

10. Once completely dry, the edges of the stuff- holders can be painted over with liquid gold leaf or the MOLOTOW Liquid Chrome marker.

Coasters in medium viscosity resin. Technology "Zephyr"

Approximate consumption of resin for 1 stuff- holder with a diameter of 11-13cm = 75 -80 g of resin. For example, 4 stuff-holders will require 300 g of medium viscosity resin, including 100 g of hardener (B) and 200 g of resin (A).

Work order:

1. Mix medium viscosity resin according to the rules. Pour the resin into four cups. Mix in them:
• any bright color 4 drops,
• white + mother of pearl
• gold leaf/sequins
• transparent resin + gloss
Start pouring the holder 20 minutes after mixing.

2. In the center of each mold, use a stick to place the gold/glitter mixed with clear resin.
3. Start pouring resin over the edges of the mold in any bright color.
4. Pour clear resin + glitter into the center.
5. After 10 minutes (after 30 minutes from the start of mixing the resin), fill in white after blue and do a few turns.
6. The resin tends to the center of the mold, forming white dots, like brains (marshmallows).

7. Go through the burner to remove bubbles.
8. After complete drying, the edges of the cup holders can be painted with liquid gold.

Coasters in medium viscosity resin. Technology "Flower"

Coasters - flowers can be made with medium viscosity resin and thick resin. I will share with you a classic version (white flower on a transparent base with sparkles in the center). By this principle, you can make any flowers, of various shapes and patterns.

Work order:

1. Prepare a mold of any size.
2. Mix medium viscosity resin according to the general principle (see section " Preparatory stage ").

For 1 stuff- holder with a diameter of 9-13 cm, you will need 60-75 grams of resin. Knead the resin directly onto the number of stuff-holders you want to make so that the color and height are the same. For example, you need 4 stuff-holders, 11cm in diameter. You will need 420 g of resin, namely

140 g of hardener (B) and 280 g of resin (A).

3. Let the resin "brew" for 25-30 minutes after mixing (if the resin is of medium viscosity). If you have a thick resin, then you need to brew for 15 minutes. The glass of resin should be warm in your hand.

4. Divide the resin into glasses:

- resin with white dye for 6 stuff-holders. You need to mix the white pigment (10 drops in resin), 20 grams per holder. In total, you need to leave 120 grams of resin.

- transparent resin mixed with sequins/gold/mother-of-pearl in the middle of the stuff-holder. It will need about 90 grams.

5. Pour the white, mixed resin into a small bag, and let sit for 15 minutes.

6. Pour clear resin over the mold immediately after mixing.

7. Go through the burner, remove the bubbles.

8. Leave the resin in the mold for 20-25 minutes!

9. Cut off the tip of the white resin dyed pouch.

10. Start drawing with a thin stream of petals from the center of the mold, try not to come off. You will have about 3-4 levels of petals. You can draw petals as you like, round, sharp, lines.

11. Go through the burner and after a while you will see how your drawing moves towards the center, forming petals.

12. You can add sparkles to the center of the picture.

Leave your stuff-holders for 24 hours. Paint the edges of the holder with liquid gold if desired. In the same way, you can make flower trays.

The colors of the petals can be any. Try to choose shades that are typical for a real flower.

Allow for the desired thickening time, otherwise, your drawing may fall to the bottom of the stuff-holder.

32. LESSON 10 "RESIN STAND"

This shelf can be used for serving sweets and other goodies.
Such a decor item will decorate an ordinary evening.

To make a two-tiered bookcase, you will need:
• silicone rubber or silicone I-GUM (see section 15. GOMMA IN PASTA)
• plexiglass, 4-5 mm wide, size 55 cm
• medium viscosity epoxy
• hardware metal
• glass chips
• see the section "Preparatory stage".

Work order:

1. Draw two arbitrary circles on plexiglass: the first circle is about 28 cm, the second 23 cm.

 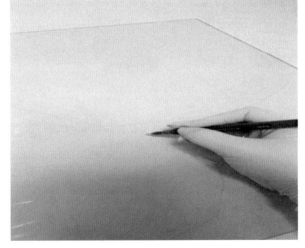

2. From silicone rubber, make the sides of the two circles that you painted on plexiglass.
3. Knead medium to heavy resin about 480 g into a 2-tiered shelf.
4. Pour a little transparent resin into a glass, pour glass chips there to rim the product.
5. Place glass chips 3 cm wide around the edges of the circles you made out of silicone.
6. Mix in 1 cup the resin with white pigment, in the 2nd cup a little gold floating powder.
7. Pour the gold-pigmented resin into the white resin.

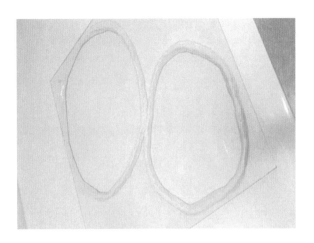
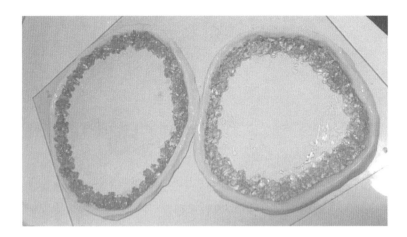

8. Without stirring start pouring the resin from the center in a circle until you finish.

9. Walk around the entire filled area with a burner. You will see the gold float to the surface.

10. Protect your products from dust.

11. After complete solidification (better in 1 day), first, remove the silicone mold. Then press down on the edge of the plexiglass to snap your circles off the glass.

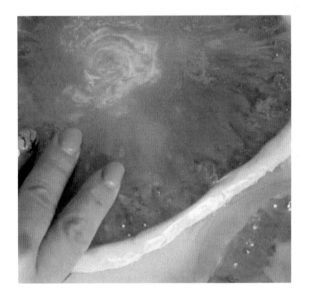

12. Mark up, find the center of your circles.

13. With Dremel, carefully drill holes for fastening the fittings.

14. Connect the fittings.

15. The edging of the bookcase can be painted with liquid gold.

After curing, allow your garment to fully polarize for another 2 days. Try to add a light (white) color to each work. It dilutes and enlivens the work.

33. LESSON 11 "RESIN VASE"

To make a vase, you will need:

• dense transparent film,
• medium viscosity epoxy resin,
• a leg for the vase (this can be a porcelain candlestick, a glass candlestick with a short stem, a glass ceiling lamp, etc.),
• glass chips
• a glass vase or something to copy the shape,
Start with preparatory work (see the section "Preparatory stage".

Work order:

1. Spread the plastic over and tape the edges to keep it from sliding off the table.
2. On the tape, draw a random circle about 28 cm.
3. Mix the resin according to the rules (see section "Preparatory stage").
4. It will take about 200g. resin per vase (Component A = 133g., Component B = 67g).
5. Mix 1 cup of stones/glass crumbs into transparent resin (30 g).
6. Lay these stones in a circle on the plastic, along the sides. Form a rim of stones approximately 4-5 cm.
7. Pour the remaining 170 g of resin into the center of the foil, according to your idea. Smear the resin with a palette knife.
8. Leave to harden for about 4-5 hours. Don't overlook the tar.
9. Prepare whatever shape you want to shape. It can be a vase, candle, jar, plate, salad bowl.

10. After 4-5 hours, carefully take the film with half-hardened resin and put the resin on top of your mold (vase/napkin holder/plate/candle), shaping the desired shape with your hands with

curved lines.

11. Once you have shaped your garment, blow a hairdryer on top of the garment, this action will remove fingerprints and the garment will regain its shine. Wear gloves while shaping the vase.

12. Leave the vase to dry completely. You can put it in the freezer for 5-10 minutes, the resin will quickly set and take the shape you gave it.

13. Remove the product from the mold and carefully remove the film from the inside.

14. Glue the upper part of the vase on the leg with glue "Second".

It is better not to use a colored film on which you will pour the resin since the resin absorbs the color of the film itself! If you are planning a vase of light colors, and the film is pink or yellow, then the resin will take over this color.

34. LESSON 12
"DECORATIVE TOYS"

Souvenir toys in any festive theme, which can be used to decorate walls, a Christmas tree, or simply put on a stand as a decoration.

You will need to create decorative toys:
• epoxy resin of medium (or thick) viscosity,
• silicone mold for chocolate (in a bakery store),
• resin pigments,
• cups and sticks for mixing resin,
• decorative stickers,
• decorative screw for jewelry,
• thin ribbon.

Work order:

1. We take resin of medium (thick) viscosity, mix according to the general principle (see the section "Preparatory stage").
2. Measure out the resin 80 g per 1 toy (Component A = 53 g, Component B = 27 g).
3. We fill our silicone molds with half a mold of one color, half a mold of a different color.
4. Use a stick or a hairdryer on medium power to mix the pattern a little. You will see how the resin will pull into the center of the mold.

 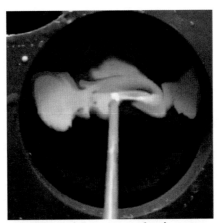 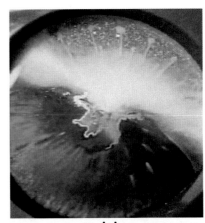

5. After the resin has completely solidified (the next day), we compose a composition on a souvenir toy. For example, you can stick stickers (New Year's, by theme, flowers, words, any letters). Fill the top with transparent resin, or resin with a little glitter.

6. From above with an awl or Dremel, carefully make a hole.
7. We screw a hook into the hole - a carnation with a loop.

8. We pass a thin ribbon or a gold rope through a narrow loop. The toy is ready.
9. You can hang on the wall, hang up nail polish, put on a stand for round objects.

You can also fill the toy with a small garland, photograph, or dried flowers. Remember that we do not fill in the resin with live or semi-dried flowers. (see the section " Bijouterie ").

35. LESSON 13 "FILL THE CUTTING BOARD"

Decorative cutting boards can be used to cut food, but cannot be cut on the resin itself. the knife will damage it. Check with the resin manufacturer that the resin has a safety hygiene certificate. The resin must be safe for contact with cold food and water (Food safety).

To fill the cutting board you will need:
• the wooden board of any shape,
• reinforced adhesive tape
• epoxy resin of medium (or thick) viscosity - 50 g,
• pigments for resin
• resin cups and sticks
• hairdryer for drawing

Work order:

1. We take the resin, mix it according to the general principle (see the section "Preparatory stage").
2. We need 50 g of resin per board (Component A = 33 g, Component B = 17 g).
3. We set our board on thick glasses, not high, and check with a level.
4. Cover the edges of the cutting board with reinforced tape. On the board, you can draw with a thin line the outlines of your fill with a simple pencil.

5. Pour resin of the same color over the part of the board that you want to paint with resin.
6. Apply the same technique of one glass, mixing several of your colors into one glass that you want to apply to your drawing.

7. Using jagged, winding lines, paint on the board these colors that you mixed into one glass.

8. Apply resin and gold in separate lines as you wish.

9. Use a medium power blow dryer to roll out the resin as desired. If the resin has run away from the desired pattern, you can use a cotton swab with alcohol.

10. Go through the burner to float the gold and remove any excess bubbles.

11. Once dry, the gold/silver lines can be applied over the resin.

Regular tape will peel off and allow the resin to pass through, so the best protection for your board is reinforced tape to protect the edges.

36. LESSON 14 "TRAY"

The functional purpose of resin trays can be different: a decorative stand on the table, for perfumes, for sweets, for candles, in the form of a cheese plate.

Wooden, glass, metal trays can be poured. You can cut your irregular shape in the form of a Geode from wood (MDF at least 3-4mm) and pour it on top. IKEA has different options for wooden trays: rotating, with handles, round, rectangular, etc.

Work order:

1. We take a resin of medium viscosity, mix according to the general principle (see the section "Preparatory stage").
2. If the tray is tall, tape the inner sides of the tray with tape just above the bottom, about 2mm.
3. Pour the resin according to the intended pattern. You can form a drawing with a palette knife, a hairdryer, or simply pouring resin from side to side.

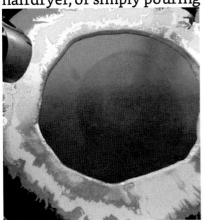

4. After finishing work, immediately remove carefully the adhesive tape from the inner sides of the tray. Do not leave overnight.
5. After the tray has completely solidified, you can apply any pattern on top of the tray. For example, you applied an even layer of glue for gilding to your hardened surface.
6. Wait for the glue to dry completely (10-15 minutes) until the "tack" state when the finger sticks to the surface but does not get dirty.
7. Apply a sheet of bead to the glue surface. Remove excess tarnishes with a hard brush.
8. Pour clear resin over the top of your drawing.

Coffee tables are poured in the same way. The only difference is that the trays have their sides. Therefore, for the tables, sides are made of scotch tape so that your edges are beautiful. (See the section "Beautiful Bumpers").

37. QUESTIONS & ANSWERS

The most popular resin questions and answers.

1. Over how many years can begin to draw resin? Is it harmful?

Recommended from the age of 15 in compliance with safety measures: respirator, nitrile gloves, ventilated room. Resin is a chemical compound with a subtle odor. Avoid getting the resin on the skin: this can lead to chemical burns and allergic reactions. Small children and pets should not be located in a room in which you work with the resin.

Resin has a cumulative effect, remember this! If today you feel good, then tomorrow you may have allergies and other unpleasant moments. Therefore, do not neglect protection, take care of your health.

2. Does the resin turn yellow?

Yes, all resins turn yellow over time, absolutely everything, even if UV protection is written. Someone is faster, someone is very slow.

If you follow some rules, you can save your products for many years.

Your resin product will not turn yellow if your product is not exposed to direct sunlight; over the radiators.

3. How many layers of resin can be poured onto the product?

The painting can be filled in at a time up to 2-3 cm (depending on the resin manufacturer). After complete drying, you can pour it again. This is how, for example, seas are done, the fill can be reached up to 8 layers.

4. Does the resin scratch? How can you protect it?

Yes, the resin is scratched. When transporting paintings, carefully wrap them in bubble wrap.

Pictures do not cover anything. If there are any scratches, you can simply re-fill the item with finishing resin.

Epoxy tables are covered with protective varnishes. Make sure the wood is well dried.

5. What is the best burner or corrector to remove bubbles?

The Ekovanna company produces such a corrector in the form of an aerosol.

The corrector removes bubbles, but the smell is quite pungent. I do not recommend working with him at home! The smell lasts a long time.

When working with a corrector, a respirator, gloves, and glasses are required so that aerosol vapors do not inhale and avoid contact with mucous membranes. You can select a manual burner for a flaming bubble (you can buy this in culinary shops).

38. CHECKLIST OF REQUIRED MATERIALS FOR A BEGINNER IN RESIN ART TECHNIQUE

Important! Protect yourself

- Mask - respirator with double filters
- Nitrile gloves
- Building glasses
- Apron + sleeves
- Work clothing that can be easily thrown away

Consumables

- Covering film for the table (dense polyethylene)
- Plastic cups (small, medium, large)
- Measuring cup (mediumm, large)
- Wet wipes containing alcohol
- Wooden spatulas (small, medium, large)
- Masking tape is durable! (wide and medium)
- Transparent containers (small, medium)
- Large tight garbage bags
- Priming (white)
- Acrylic paints
- Artboards (round, square, rectangular, hexagons, Geoda blanks)
- Brushes (art, construction)
- Roller (smalll, medium)
- Belinka
- Silicone in pistols
- Surface protection film

Tools

- Industrial Hair Dryer
- Household hair dryer
- Construction level
- Electronic scales (can be household)
- Sander (eccentric) + discs (40 to 1800) + felt polishing disc + sanding sheets

- Jigsaw (not for a beginner)
- Dremel + accessories
- Touch burner + gas can
- Scissors
- Stationery knife

Resins

- Epoxy Jewelry Resin
- Pigments for resins
- Additives, mediums
- Resin cleaner
- Pop-up powders
- Resi-wave

Elements

- Texture paste
- Potal (liquid, sheet) + glue
- POSCA resistant glass markers
- Mirror crumb
- Colored pebbles
- Glitters, sequins, snowflakes, holographic mirror powder
- Natural stones
- Chameleon paper
- Acrylic paints
- Alcohol ink
- Itten's color wheel

P.S. It is not necessary to buy everything at once, you can find some of the materials at home, some borrow until you understand that this is for you.

39. PICTURE SET FOR INSPIRATION

Small natural Pictures of the inspiration for the creation of Geodes, sea, space, and marble.

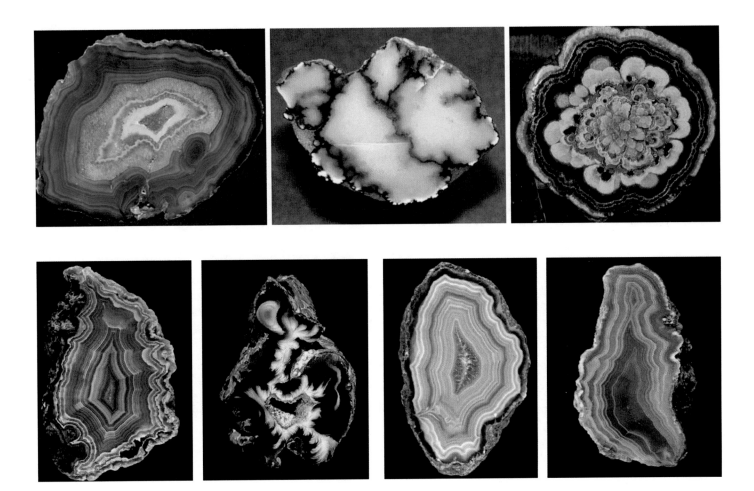

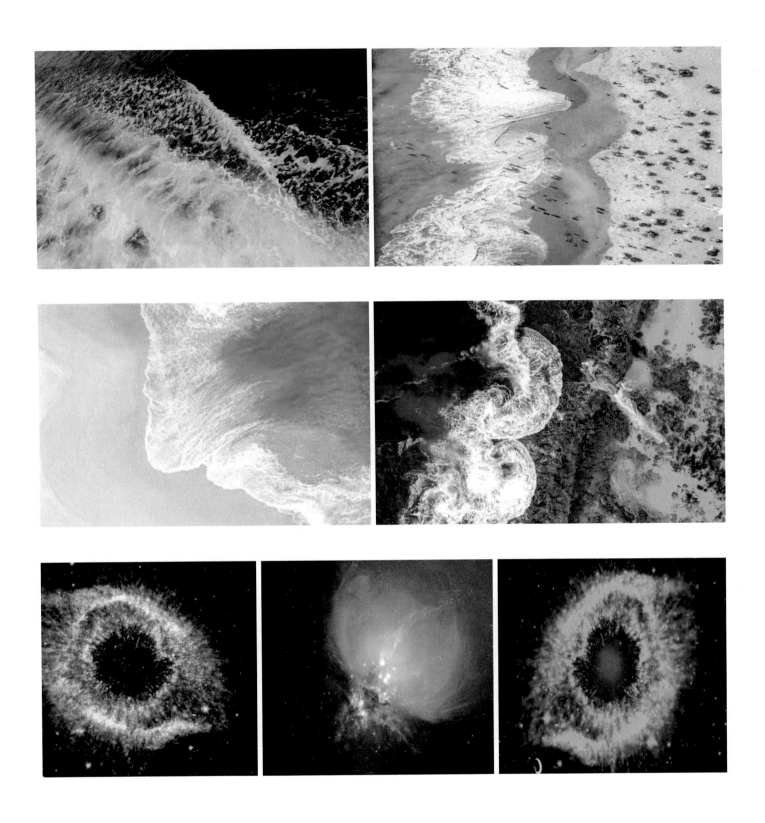

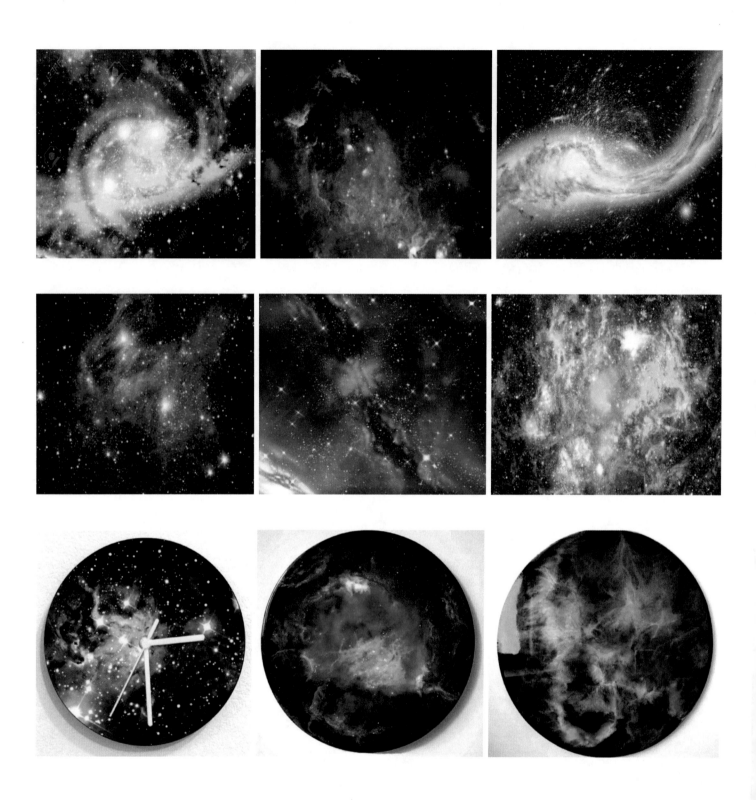

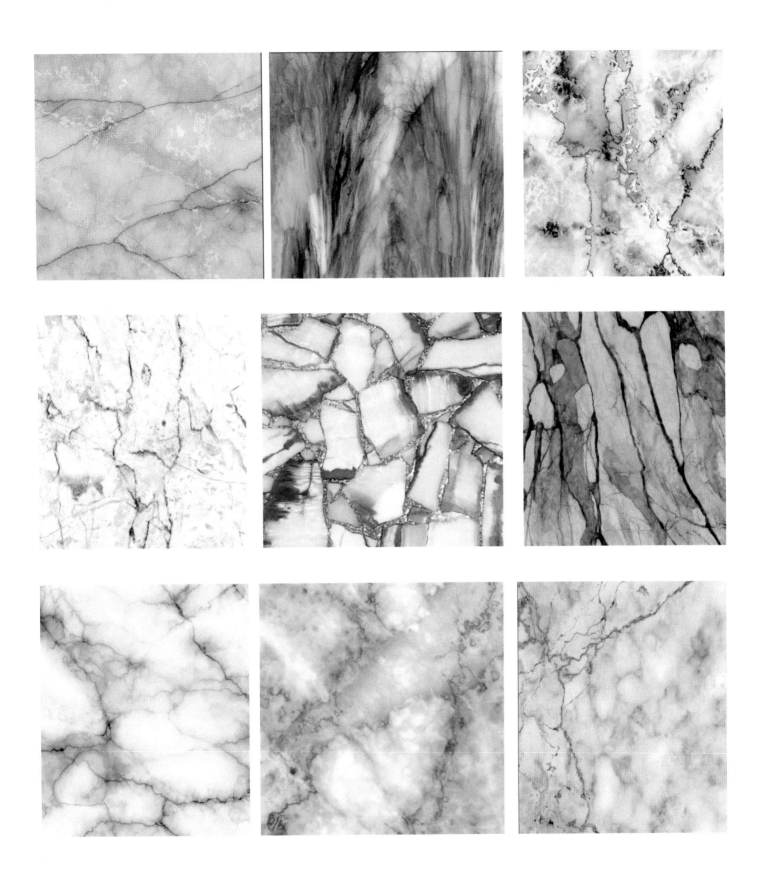

40. BOOKS AND FILMS ABOUT ART.

5 books on art that resonated in me

1. Julia Cameron. The Artist's Way.

Will teach you to think creatively.

2. Anastasia Postrigai. Fall in love with art.

From Rembrandt to Andy Warhol.

3. Sam Phillips. ... Isms . Understanding Modern Art.

A guide to the world of art. Acquaintance with art, for beginners.

4. Elena Truskova. Inspiration: how to allow yourself to create.

Finding inspiration.

5. Johannes Itten. The Art of Color.

This book is called the Bible of Colors. The basics of color combinations.

6 films about art

"Frida" (2002)
"Genius" (TV series 2017)
"Big Eyes" (2014)
"Masterpiece" (2018)
"Van Gogh. With love, Vincent "(cartoon 2017)
"Klimt" (2005)

41. COLOR SCHEMES FOR PICTURES

I use color schemes generator by www.coolors.co. It can create the perfect palette or get inspired by thousands of beautiful color schemes.

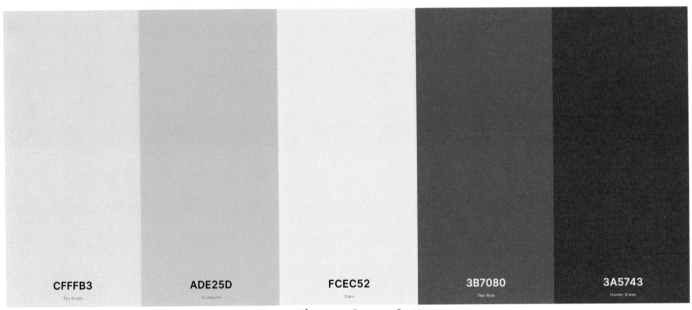

| CFFFB3 | ADE25D | FCEC52 | 3B7080 | 3A5743 |
| Tea Green | Inchworm | Corn | Teal Blue | Hunter Green |

Trending color palettes

Get inspired by thousands of beautiful color
schemes and make something cool!

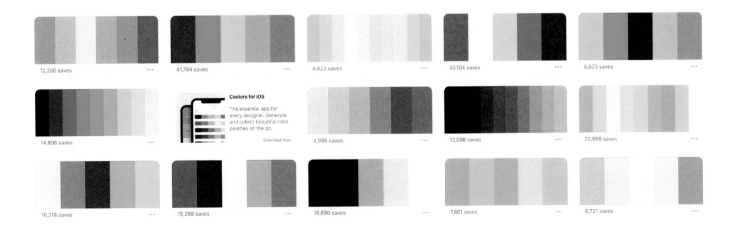

Color circle is also very useful tool to choose a combination of colors in the interior pictures. I use it on www.galactic.ink/sphere/.

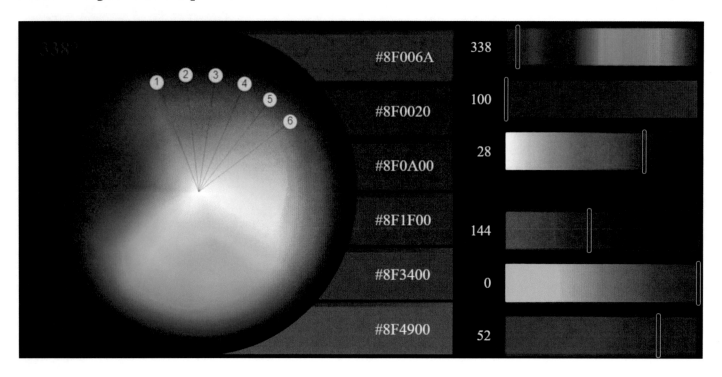

ABOUT THE AUTHOR

Tatiana Danilova

My name is Tatiana Danilova. I am an artist and teacher, and also founder of the Artan studio in Ljubljana (Slovenia).

The new country allowed me to do what I love - namely to create modern paintings and decorative objects in different techniques (Fluid Art, Resin Art, Alcohol Ink) and materials (watercolor, acrylic, resin, ink, potal, decorative paste).

I have a craving for everything beautiful and art since childhood. I painted with watercolors, liners, but most of all I am fascinated by interesting and bizarre forms of resin and alcohol ink.

Attending many master-classes and courses, by famous artists in Moscow and St. Petersburg, I studied Resin Art, Fluid Art, and Alcohol Ink techniques In September 2019, my works were presented at the international exhibition 2.ART Expo Ljubljana.

I invite you to become acquainted with my work, useful posts, and video reviews:
Instagram - @artanslo
Facebook - @artanstudioslo
Website – www.artan-studio.com

Made in the USA
Monee, IL
29 July 2021